THE MINISTRY OF
Intercessory Prayer

ANDREW MURRAY

BETHANYHOUSE
Minneapolis, Minnesota

The Ministry of Intercessory Prayer
by Andrew Murray

Copyright © 1981, 2003
Bethany House Publishers

Originally published in 1897 under the title *The Ministry of Intercession.*
Published previously by Bethany House Publishers as *The Ministry of Intercessory Prayer.*
Newly edited and updated for today's reader by Nancy Renich.

Cover design by Cheryl Neisen/Eric Walljasper

Published by Bethany House Publishers
11400 Hampshire Avenue South
Bloomington, Minnesota 55438

Bethany House Publishers is a division of
Baker Publishing Group, Grand Rapids, Michigan.

Printed in the United States of America

Library of Congress Cataloging-in-Publication Data

Murray, Andrew, 1828–1917.
    The ministry of intercessory prayer / by Andrew Murray.
       p. cm.
Rev. ed. of: The ministry of intercession. 1897.
    ISBN 0-7642-2763-7 (pbk.)
    1. Intercessory prayer—Christianity. I. Murray, Andrew, 1828–1917. Ministry of intercession. II. Title.
BV210.3 .M85   2003
248.3'2—dc21   2002152840

TO

My brethren in the ministry

and

other laborers in the Gospel,

this volume

is affectionately inscribed.

ANDREW MURRAY was born in South Africa in 1828. After receiving his education in Scotland and Holland, he returned to Africa and spent many years as a missionary pastor. He and his wife, Emma, raised eight children. He is best known for his many devotional books, including some of the most enduring classics of Christian literature.

Contents

There are noble Christian workers,
  The men of faith and power,
The overcoming wrestlers
  Of many a midnight hour;
Prevailing princes with their God,
  Who will not be denied,
Who bring down showers of blessing
  To swell the rising tide.
The Prince of Darkness quaileth
  At their triumphant way,
Their fervent prayer availeth
  To sap his subtle sway.

—Frances R. Havergal

Introduction

A friend who heard this book would be published, asked what the difference would be between it and my previous one, *With Christ in the School of Prayer* (*Teach Me to Pray*, 2002). An answer to that question may be the best introduction I can give to this volume.

Any acceptance the former work has had must be attributed to the prominence given to two great truths: (1) *Jesus taught that you can ask and receive what you will.* (2) *Persevering prayer can prevail and obtain what God at first could not and would not give.*

Some people have the idea that to ask and expect an answer is not the highest form of prayer. They argue that fellowship with God, apart from requests, is greater than supplication. They argue that petition contains something of selfishness and bargaining, and to worship is more than to ask for things.

Others insist that prayer is often unanswered. They think more of the spiritual benefit derived from the *exercise* of prayer than the actual gifts or answers obtained.

I admit a measure of truth is to be found in both of these views. However, *With Christ in the School of Prayer* points out how our Lord continually spoke of prayer as a means of obtaining what we desire, and how He seeks in every possible way to awaken in us the confident expectation of an answer. I showed how prayer, by which we enter into the mind of God, asserts the royal power of a renewed will. It brings about on earth that which without prayer could not have been accomplished. Power in prayer is the highest proof of our being made in the likeness of God's Son.

We are found worthy of entering into fellowship with God not only in adoration and worship but also in being instrumental in the rule of the world. In this manner we become the intelligent channel through which God can fulfill His eternal purpose. I sought to reiterate and reinforce the precious truth Christ preached continually: The blessing of prayer is that you can ask and receive what you will. The highest exercise and glory of prayer is that persevering boldness can prevail and obtain what God at first could not and would not give.

Many people question, "But if the answer to prayer is so positively promised, why are there so many unanswered prayers?" Christ taught us that the answer depended upon certain conditions. He spoke of faith, of perseverance, of praying in His name, of praying according to the will of God. But all these conditions were summed up in one truth: "If you remain in me and my words remain in you, ask whatever you wish, and it will be given you" (John 15:7).

It became clear that the power to pray the effectual prayer of faith depends upon our *life in Christ*. We must commit ourselves to live as entirely in Christ and for Christ as the branch lives in the vine. Then these promises will be true for us. "On that day," Christ said of the day of Pentecost, "you will ask in my name." Only a life full of the Holy Spirit can know the true power to ask in Christ's name. This led to emphasizing the truth that the ordinary Christian life cannot appropriate these promises. It needs a sound and vigorous spiritual life to pray in power. This teaching in turn led to emphasizing the need of a life of entire consecration. Several have told me how in reading the first book they saw for the first time what a better life could be lived—and must be lived—if Christ's promises are to be effectual in our lives.

With regard to these truths, the present volume does not waver. I only desire that they are enforced with enough clarity to help every Christian who reads these words to comprehend the reality and the glory of our privilege as God's children: "Ask whatever you wish, and it will be given you" (John 15:7).

This book owes its existence to my desire to enforce two more truths, of which I had no such previous understanding: (1) *Christ meant prayer to be the great power by which His church should do its work, and the neglect of prayer is the reason the church lacks greater power.* (2) *We have far too little understanding of the place that intercession (as distinguished from prayer for ourselves) ought to have in the church and in the Christian life.*

In the first chapter I state how my convictions about this have been strengthened, and what inspired me to write about it. It is meant to be, on behalf of all God's people (including myself), a confession of shortcomings and of sin. At the same time it is a call to believe that things can be different, and that Christ waits to enable us by His Spirit to pray as He wants us to pray.

There is a life in the Spirit, a life of abiding in Christ, within our reach. In that life the power of prayer can be realized in a measure that we could not have thought possible before—both the power to pray and the power to obtain an answer to our prayers. Any failure in our prayer life, any desire or hope to obtain the place Christ has prepared for us, brings us to the very root of the doctrine of grace. Only by a full surrender to a life of abiding in the Vine, by yielding to the fullness of the Spirit's leading, can our prayer life be restored to a healthy state. I feel I have inadequately expressed this. And I trust that God, who chooses the weak things, will use this volume for His glory.

Our King is glorified in intercession; and we too will find our highest glory in it. Through it He continues His saving work; in fact, He can do nothing without it. It is our instrument to impart spiritual blessing to others. The power of the church to bless rests on intercession. When, due to lack of teaching or spiritual insight, we trust in our own diligence and efforts to influence the world, and work more than we pray, the presence and power of God will not be seen in our work as they should be.

Such thoughts have led me to wonder how I can stir believers to a sense of their high calling in this, and how to help and train them to take part in it. And so this book differs from the former in its attempt to invite all who have never taken a systematic part in the great work of intercession to begin and give themselves to it.

There are numerous ministers of the Gospel who have known and are proving what prayer can do. But there are numbers of others who carry on their work with little prayer and as many more who do not pray at all because they do not know how to or where to begin. I desire to persuade them all to join the host of intercessors who are bringing down the blessings of heaven to earth. For their sakes, and for others who need help, I have prepared helps and tips for a thirty-day school of intercession toward the end of the book, called "Pray Without Ceasing."

I have asked those who would join in this work to begin by giving at least ten minutes a day. By doing anything, we learn how to do it. As we take hold and begin, God's Spirit will help us. As we daily hear God's call and put it into practice, the realization will awaken in us: *I am an intercessor*. We will also sense the need of living in Christ and being full of the Spirit in order to do this work in the correct way. Nothing will so test and stimulate the Christian life as the honest attempt to be an intercessor.

It is difficult to conceive how much the church and we will gain if with our whole heart we accept this position of honor that God offers us. I am confident that the first month's course in the school of intercession will awaken us to how little we know on the subject. A second and third month may only deepen our sense of lack and unfitness. The confession "We do not know what to pray for as we ought" is the prerequisite to the experience "The Spirit ... makes intercession for the saints" (Romans 8: 26–27 NKJV). Our sense of ignorance will lead us to depend upon the Spirit's praying in us and to feel our need of living in the Spirit.

We have heard a great deal about systematic Bible study, and we praise God for the many Bible classes and studies that meet in the churches and in homes. The leaders of such classes should look into beginning *prayer* classes as well—helping their students to pray in private, and training them to be people of prayer above all else.

Faith in God's Word can nowhere be so exercised and perfected as in the intercession that asks of God and expects an answer. Throughout Scripture, in the life of every saint and of

God's own Son, throughout the history of the church, God is, first of all, a prayer-hearing God. Let us try to help God's children to know their God, and encourage all God's servants to labor with this assurance: *The primary and most blessed part of my work is to ask and receive from my Father what I can give to others.*

Now you see that this book is the confirmation and the call to put into practice the two lessons of the former one: Ask, and it will be given to you; and meeting the conditions that God requires to find Him in the place of prayer. A life that abides in Christ and is filled with the Spirit is a life committed as a branch to the work of the Vine. It has the power to claim these promises and to pray the "effectual prayer that avails much." Lord, teach us all to pray.

—Andrew Murray

Chapter 1

The Lack of Prayer

You do not have, because you do not ask God.

James 4:2b

He saw that there was no man, and wondered that there was no intercessor.

Isaiah 59:16 NKJV

No one calls on your name or strives to lay hold of you.

Isaiah 64:7

At our last Wellington Convention for the Deepening of the Spiritual Life, the morning meetings were devoted to prayer and intercession. Great blessing was enjoyed both in listening to what the Word teaches on the subject and in joining together in united supplication. Many voiced the opinion that we know too little of persistent prayer and that it is indeed one of the greatest needs of the church.

I have recently attended a number of conventions. At a Dutch Missionary Conference at Langlaagte, prayer was the subject of the messages. At another in Johannesburg, a businessman said it was his deep conviction that more of the spirit and practice of intercession was what the church of our day greatly needed. Later at a Dutch Ministerial Conference, we spent two days on the work of the Holy Spirit and then three days on the relationship of the Spirit to prayer. Everywhere people confessed, "We pray too little!" Along with this, there seemed to be a consensus that because of the pressure of work and deep-rooted habits, it was almost impossible to hope for any significant change.

These conversations made a deep impression on me. There appeared to be such hopelessness on the part of God's servants as to the possibility of change with regard to their prayer habits. This attitude must surely hinder our joy in God and our power in His service. I prayed that God would give me words to address the dilemma, but even more to stir up faith and inspire the assurance that God by His Spirit *can and will enable us to pray as we ought.*

I will cite some examples that show how the lack of an adequate prayer life is universal.

Last year in a message to ministers, Dr. Whyte of Free St. George's, Edinburgh, said that as a young minister he thought that any time left over from pastoral visitation should be spent in his study with his books. He wanted to feed his people with the very best he could prepare for them. But now he was learning that *prayer* was more important than *study.* He reminded the brethren of the election of deacons to take charge of the collections: that the twelve might "give [them]selves continually to prayer and to the ministry of the word" (Acts 6:4 NKJV). He said that at times when the deacons gave him his salary, he had to ask himself whether he had been as faithful in his obligations as the deacons had been in theirs. Finally, he urged his brethren to pray more. What a solemn confession and warning from one of our pastors.

During the Regent Square Convention, the subject came up in conversation with a well-known London minister. He insisted that if so much time must be given to prayer, it would mean the neglect of the other duties of his post: "There is the morning mail, before breakfast, with ten or twelve letters that *must* be answered. Then there are committee meetings waiting, with countless other engagements, more than enough to fill up the day. It is difficult to see how extended prayer can be fit in."

I answered that it was simply a question of whether the call of God for our time and attention was more important than that of man. If God was waiting to meet us and to give us blessing and power from above for His work, it was certainly a short-sighted policy to put other work ahead of time with God in prayer.

At one of our ministerial meetings, the superintendent of a large district stated, "In the morning I have half an hour with God in the Word and in prayer before breakfast. After I go out, I am occupied all day with numerous engagements, but I do not think many minutes elapse without my breathing a prayer for guidance or help. After my day's work, I have my evening devotions and speak to God of the day's work. But of the intense, definite, importunate prayer of which Scripture speaks, I know little."

We all see the contrast between a man whose income barely maintains his family and keeps up his business, and a man whose income enables him to expand his business and also help others. There may be an earnest Christian life that has just enough prayer to maintain the position already attained to, but without much further spiritual growth in Christlikeness. The former is more of a defensive attitude, seeking to fight off temptation, rather than an aggressive one that reaches after higher attainment. If we desire to grow from strength to strength and to experience God's power in sanctification and blessing on others, we must be more persevering in prayer. The Scripture's teaching about crying to God day and night, continuing steadfastly in prayer, watching unto prayer, and being heard for our importunity, must in some degree become our experience if we are to become intercessors.

The same question was put in a somewhat different form at the next convention: "I am at the head of a parish, with a large outlying district to care for. I see the importance of extended prayer, and yet my life hardly allows time for it. Are we to give in to the situation? Tell us how we can attain to what we truly desire in the area of prayer."

I conceded that the difficulty was universal.

One of our most honored South African missionaries had the same complaint: "At five in the morning people are at my door waiting for medicine. At six the printers come, and I have to get their work set up and guide them in some areas of which they are not familiar. At nine the school calls me, and until late at night I am kept busy with letters to answer."

In my response to this brother, I quoted a Dutch proverb: " 'What *is* heaviest must *weigh* heaviest'—must have the first place. The law of God is unchangeable; as on earth, so in our communication with heaven, we only get as we give. Unless we are willing to pay the price, to sacrifice time and attention and seemingly legitimate or necessary tasks for the sake of the spiritual gifts, we need not look for much power from above in our work."

The whole group was united in the same confession. It had been thought over; it had been mourned over, times without number. Still, there they were, all these pressing claims and failures of resolves to pray more barring the way to success.

Let me call one more witness. During my trip I met one of the Cowley Fathers, who held retreats for clergy of the Church of England. I was interested to hear the line of teaching he followed. In the course of conversation, he used the expression "the distraction of business," which he said was one of the great difficulties he had to deal with. By the vows of his Order, he was bound to give himself especially to prayer. But he found it very difficult. Every day he had to be in four different areas of the town he lived in; his predecessor had left him the responsibility of several committees, where he was expected to do virtually all the work. It seemed everything conspired to keep him from prayer.

Surely this testimony proves that prayer does not have the place it should have in our ministerial and Christian life. The shortcoming is one that all willingly confess. These examples also reveal that the difficulties blocking deliverance make a return to a true and full prayer life almost impossible.

But thanks be to God, "The things which are impossible with men are possible with God!" (Luke 18:27 NKJV). "God is able to make all grace abound toward you; that you, always having all sufficiency in all things, may abound to every good work" (2 Corinthians 9:8 NKJV).

God's call to much prayer need not be a burden or cause for continual self-condemnation. He intends it to be a joyful task. He can make it an inspiration. Through it He can give us strength for all our work and bring blessing to others by His power that works in us.

Without hesitation, let us confess our sin of neglect and confront it in the name of our Mighty Redeemer. *The same light that shows us our sin and condemns us for it will show us the way out of it, into a life of liberty that pleases God.* Let our lack of prayer convict us of the coolness in our Christian life that lies at the root of it. God will use the discovery to bring us not only the power to pray that we long for but also the joy of a new and healthy life of which prayer is the spontaneous expression.

How can inactive prayer be transformed into action? How can it be supercharged into the power by which evil might be conquered? How can our relationship with the Father become what it ought to be—one of continual prayer and intercession—so that the world around us will be blessed of God?

We must begin by going back to God's Word and studying what place God intends prayer to have in the life of His child and of His church. A fresh understanding of what prayer is *according to the will of God*, and of what our prayers can be *through the grace of God*, will free us from our weak and impaired attitudes concerning the absolute necessity of diligent and regular prayer.

As we gain insight into how reasonable and right this divine appointment is, and as we are fully convinced of how wonderfully it fits in with God's love and our own happiness, we shall be freed from the false impression of its being an arbitrary demand. With our whole heart and soul we will agree and yield to it and rejoice in it as the one and only way for the blessing of God to come to earth. All thought of task and burden, of self-effort and strain, will pass away. As simple as breathing is in the healthy physical life, so should praying be in the Christian life that is led and filled by the Spirit of God.

As we think about this teaching of God's Word on prayer, and accept it, we will see how failure in our prayer life results from failure in our life in the Spirit. Prayer is one of the most natural and joyous functions of the Spirit-filled life. How can we expect to fulfill a life of prayer that pleases God without our soul being in perfect health and our life possessed and moved by God's Spirit?

Fresh insight into the place God intends prayer to have in a full Christian life will show us that we have not been living the true and abundant life. Any thought of praying more or of praying more effectively will be in vain unless we are brought into closer intimacy with our blessed Lord Jesus. Christ is our life. He lives in us in such reality that His life of prayer on earth and His intercession in heaven are breathed into us in the measure that our surrender and our faith allow.

Jesus Christ is the Healer of all our diseases, the Conqueror of all our enemies, and the Deliverer from all our sin. Our failure should teach us to turn afresh to Him, to find in Him the grace He gives to pray as we ought. The humiliation of our lack may be transformed into our greatest blessing. Pray that God will visit our souls and fit us for the work of intercession, which is the greatest need of the church and of the world. Only by intercession can that power be brought down from heaven that will enable the church to overcome the world and win souls for Christ.

Stir up the latent gift that remains unused. Seek to gather and train and band together as many as you can to be God's reminders. Nothing but persistent, believing prayer can meet the onslaught of the spirit of worldliness that is reported everywhere.

Chapter 2

The Ministry of the Spirit and Prayer

"If you then, though you are evil, know how to give good gifts to your children, how much more will your Father in heaven give the Holy Spirit to those who ask him!"

Luke 11:13

Christ had just said (11:9), "Ask and it will be given to you"; God's giving is inseparably connected with our asking. He applies this principle especially to the gift of the Holy Spirit. As surely as a father on earth gives bread to his child, so God gives the Holy Spirit to them that ask Him. One great law rules the whole ministry of the Spirit: *We must ask; God must give.* When the Holy Spirit was poured out at Pentecost with a flow that never ceases, it was in answer to prayer. His inflow into the believer's heart and His outflow in rivers of living water always depend upon the law "Ask and it will be given to you."

Along with our confession of our lack of prayer, we also need a clear understanding of the place prayer occupies in God's plan of redemption. Nowhere is this clearer than in the first half of the book of Acts. The outpouring of the Holy Spirit at the birth of the church and the first freshness of its heavenly life in the power of that Spirit will teach us how *prayer on earth, whether as cause or effect, is the true measure of the presence of the Spirit of heaven.*

We begin with the well-known words "These all continued with one accord in prayer and supplication." And then follows: "When the day of Pentecost came, they were all together in one place. All of them were filled with the Holy Spirit. Those who accepted his message were baptized, and about three thousand were added to their number that day" (Acts 2:1, 4; 2:41).

The great work of redemption had been accomplished. Christ had promised the coming of the Holy Spirit. He sat down on His throne and received the Spirit from the Father. But all this was not enough. One more thing was needed: ten days of united, continued supplication of the disciples.

Intense, continued prayer prepared the disciples' hearts, opened the windows of heaven, and brought down the promised gift. The power of the Spirit could not be given without Christ sitting on the throne, but neither could it descend without the fervent, persistent prayer of the disciples.

Here at the birth of the church, the law is laid down for all ages that no matter what else may be found on earth, the power of the Spirit must be prayed down from heaven. The measure of continued believing prayer will be the measure of the Spirit's working in the church.

Direct, definite, determined prayer is what we need. This is confirmed in Acts, chapter 4. Peter and John had been brought before the Council and threatened with punishment. When they returned to their brethren and reported what had been said to them, "they raised their voices together to God in prayer," and prayed for boldness to speak the Word. "After they had prayed, the place where they were meeting was shaken . . . and they were all filled with the Holy Spirit and spoke the word of God boldly. All the believers were one in heart and mind. . . . With great power the apostles continued to testify to the resurrection of the Lord Jesus, and much grace was upon them all."

It is as if the experience of Pentecost is repeated a second time over—with the prayer, the shaking of the house, the filling with the Spirit, the speaking of God's Word with boldness and power, the great grace that was upon all, the manifestation of unity and love—all in order to imprint permanently on the heart of the church that *it is prayer that lies at the root of the spiritual life and power of the church*. The degree with which God gives His Spirit is determined by the insistence of our asking. He gives as a father to the one who asks as a child.

In the sixth chapter of Acts, we find that when people complained about the neglect of the Grecian Jews in the distribution of alms, the apostles proposed the appointment of deacons to serve the tables. They said, "We . . . will give our attention to prayer and the ministry of the word." It is often and rightly said that there is nothing in honest business (kept in its place as entirely subordinate to the kingdom, which must always be first) that should prevent fellowship with God. Least of all, should ministering to the poor hinder the spiritual life, and yet the apostles felt it would hinder their giving themselves to the ministry of prayer and the Word.

What does this teach? The maintenance of the spirit of prayer is possible in many kinds of work, but it is not enough for those who are the leaders of the church. To communicate with the King on the throne and keep the heavenly world in clear and fresh focus; to draw down the power and blessing of that world not only for the maintenance of our own spiritual life but also for those around us; to receive continual instruction and empowerment for the great work to be done—the apostles, as ministers of the Word, felt the need to be free from other duties that they might give themselves to extended prayer.

James writes, "Religion that God our Father accepts as pure and faultless is this: to look after orphans and widows in their distress and to keep oneself from being polluted by the world" (1:27). If ever any work were a sacred one, it was that of caring for these Grecian widows. Still, even such duties might interfere with the special call to give themselves to prayer and the ministry of the Word. On earth, as in heaven, there is power in the division of labor. Some, like the deacons, had primarily to serve tables and administer the offerings of the church here on earth. Others had to be freed for that steadfast continuance in prayer that would secure the constant flow of power from above.

The minister of Christ is set apart to give himself as much to prayer as to the ministry of the Word. Faithful obedience to this law is the secret of the church's power and success. Before, just as after Pentecost, the apostles were men given over to prayer.

In chapter 8 of Acts, we have the intimate connection between the Pentecostal gift and prayer from another point of view. At Samaria, Philip had preached with great blessing, and many had believed. But the Holy Spirit had not yet fallen on any of them. The apostles sent down Peter and John to pray for them that they might receive the Holy Spirit.

The power for such prayer was a higher gift than preaching. It was the work of men who had been in closest contact with the Lord. It was a work that was essential to the perfection of the life that preaching and baptism, faith and conversion had only begun. Of all the gifts of the early church to which we should aspire, there is none more needed than the gift of prayer—prayer that brings the Holy Spirit into the midst of believers. This power is given to those who say, "We will give ourselves to prayer."

The outpouring of the Holy Spirit in the house of Cornelius at Caesarea provides another testimony to the wonderful inter-dependence of prayer and the Spirit—another proof of what will come to those who give themselves to prayer.

Peter went up at midday to pray on the housetop. He saw heaven opened and a vision that revealed to him the cleansing of the Gentiles. Then followed the message of the three men from Cornelius, a man who "prayed always," and had heard from an angel, "Your prayers are come up before God." Then the voice of the Spirit was heard saying, "Go with them."

It was to a praying Peter that the will of God was revealed, to whom guidance was given to go to Caesarea. There he was brought into contact with a praying and prepared company of hearers. No wonder that in answer to all this prayer, blessing beyond all expectation came and the Holy Spirit was poured out upon the Gentiles.

A minister who is given to prayer will have access to God's will of which he would otherwise know nothing. He will find praying people where he does not expect them. He will receive blessing above all he asks or thinks. The teaching and the power of the Holy Spirit are unalterably linked to prayer.

The power that the church's prayer has with its glorified King is shown not only as the apostles prayed but also as the Christian community prays. In chapter 12 of Acts, we have the story of Peter in prison on the eve of his execution. The death of James had aroused the church to a sense of great danger; the thought of losing Peter, too, awakened all its energies: "So Peter was kept in prison, but the church was earnestly praying to God for him" (Acts 12:5).

That prayer was effective. Peter was delivered. When he came to the house of Mary, he found "many people had gathered and were praying." Stone walls and double chains, soldiers and guards, and then the iron gate—all gave way before the power from heaven that prayer brought down to effect his rescue. The whole power of the Roman Empire, as represented by Herod, was impotent in the presence of the power that the church of the Holy Spirit wielded in prayer.

Those Christians stood in close and vital relationship with their Lord. They knew well the words "All authority in heaven and on earth has been given to me" and "Surely I am with you always, to the very end of the age" (Matthew 28:18–20) were absolutely true. They had faith in His promise to hear whatever they asked. Undergirded by these things, they prayed in the assurance that the powers of heaven not only could work on earth but that they would work at the church's request and on its behalf. The church at Pentecost believed in prayer and practiced it.

For one more illustration of the place and the blessing of prayer among men filled with the Holy Spirit, chapter 13 of Acts names five men at Antioch who dedicated themselves to ministering to the Lord by prayer and fasting. Their praying was not in vain, because as they ministered to the Lord, the Holy Spirit met them and gave them new insight into God's plans. He called them to be fellow workers with himself. There was a work to which He had called Barnabas and Saul. The part and privilege of the five men would be to separate Barnabas and Saul with renewed fasting and prayer and to let them go, "sent on their way by the Holy Spirit."

God would not send forth His chosen servants without the cooperation of His church. Men on earth were to have a partnership in the work of God. Prayer fitted and prepared them for this. To praying men, the Holy Spirit gave authority to do His work and use His name. It was through prayer that the Holy Spirit was given. Prayer is still the only secret of true church extension, prayer that is guided from heaven to find and send forth people who are called by God and anointed by the Spirit.

In answer to prayer, the Holy Spirit will show those who He has selected; in response to prayer that sets them apart under His guidance, He will give the honor of knowing that they are "sent on their way by the Holy Spirit." Prayer links the King on the throne with the church at His feet. The church, the human link, receives its divine strength from the power of the Holy Spirit, who comes in answer to their prayers.

In these chapters on the history of the church at Pentecost, two great truths stand out: *Where there is much prayer, there will be much of the Spirit; where there is much of the Spirit, there will be ever-increasing prayer*. So clear is the living connection between the two that when the Spirit is given in answer to prayer, it stimulates more prayer to prepare for a fuller revelation and communication of His divine power and grace. If prayer was the power by which the early church flourished and triumphed, wouldn't it be the one need of the church of our day?

Let us learn what ought to be counted as principles in the work of the church:

1. Heaven still has a full store of spiritual blessing just as it did then.
2. God still delights to give the Holy Spirit to them that ask Him.
3. Our life and work are still as dependent on the direct impartation of divine power as the disciples' were at the time of Pentecost.
4. Prayer is still the appointed means for drawing down heavenly blessings in power upon all the church.
5. God still seeks for men and women who will, together with all their other work, give themselves to persevering prayer.

We have the privilege of offering ourselves to God to labor in prayer for the blessings He has in store for the church. Shouldn't we beseech God to make this truth live in us? And implore Him that we will not rest until we count the practice of intercession our highest privilege? It is the only certain means of obtaining blessing for the church, the world, and our own lives.

Chapter 3

A Model of Intercession

Then he said to them, "Suppose one of you has a friend, and he goes to him at midnight and says, 'Friend, lend me three loaves of bread, because a friend of mine on a journey has come to me, and I have nothing to set before him.'

"Then the one inside answers, 'Don't bother me. The door is already locked, and my children are with me in bed. I can't get up and give you anything.'

"I tell you, though he will not get up and give him the bread because he is his friend, yet because of the man's boldness he will get up and give him as much as he needs."

Luke 11:5–8

I have posted watchmen on your walls, O Jerusalem; they will never be silent day or night. You who call on the LORD, give yourselves no rest, and give him no rest till he establishes Jerusalem and makes her the praise of the earth.

Isaiah 62:6–7

We have now seen the power prayer has. It is the one power on earth that commands the power of heaven. The story of the early days of the church is God's great object lesson to teach His church today what prayer can do. Prayer alone can pull down the treasures and powers of heaven to our life on earth.

Remember the lessons we learned of how prayer is at once indispensable and irresistible:

1. Unknown and untold power and blessing is stored up for us in heaven.
2. That power will make us a blessing to others and equip us to do any work or face any danger.
3. This power and blessing is to be sought in prayer continually and persistently.
4. Those who have tapped the heavenly power can pray it down upon others.
5. In all the relationships between ministers and laypeople, in all the ministries of Christ's church, prayer is the secret of success.
6. Prayer can defy all the power of the world and equip us to conquer that world for Christ.
7. The power of the heavenly life, the power of God's own Spirit, and the power of Omnipotence waits for prayer to bring it down.

In true, unselfish prayer there is little thought of personal need or happiness. Rather, there is a desire to witness for Christ and bring Him and His salvation to others. It was the thought of God's kingdom and glory that possessed the disciples. If we would be delivered from the sin of limiting prayer, we must enlarge our hearts for the work of intercession.

To pray constantly only for ourselves is a mark of failure in prayer. It is in intercession for others that our faith and love and perseverance will be stirred up and that the power of the Spirit will be found to equip us for bringing salvation to people. How can we become more faithful and successful in prayer? See again in the parable of the friend at midnight (Luke 11) how the Master teaches us that intercession for the needy is the highest exercise of believing and prevailing prayer. Intercession is the most perfect form of prayer. It is the prayer Christ prays from His throne. Here are the elements of true intercession:

1. *Urgent need.* Intercession has its origin at the point of need. The friend came at midnight, an untimely hour. He had a guest and could not buy bread. If we are to learn to pray as we should, we must open our eyes and heart to the needs around us.

We hear continually of the millions living in spiritual darkness, perishing for lack of the Bread of Life. We hear also of millions of nominal Christians, the great majority of them almost as ignorant and indifferent as those in unreached countries. We see millions more in the Christian church, not ignorant or indifferent perhaps, yet knowing little of a walk in the light of God or of the power of a life fed by the bread of heaven. Each of us has our own circle—congregation, school, friends, Bible study—in which the general complaint is that the light and life of God are little known. But if we believe what we profess, that God alone is able to help, that God will certainly help in answer to prayer, all this ought to make intercessors of us. It should motivate us to be people who give their lives to prayer for those in their sphere of influence.

Let us face up to and consider the need: each Christless soul going down into outer darkness, perishing of hunger, while there is bread enough and to spare! Millions each year die without the knowledge of Christ! Our own neighbors and friends, souls entrusted to us, die without hope! Christians around us live sickly, weak, fruitless lives! Surely prayer is needed. Nothing but prayer to God for help will avail.

2. *Willing love.* The friend took his friend into his house and into his heart. He laid aside the fact that he was already in bed with his family. At midnight he got up and went to his cupboard to find bread and perhaps something to go with it for his friend and the friend's guest. He sacrificed an undisturbed night of rest and his own comfort to find the needed provision. Love "seeks not her own." It is the very nature of love to give up and forget itself for the sake of others. It takes their needs and makes them its own. It finds its real joy in living and dying for others, as Christ did.

The love of a mother for her prodigal son makes her pray for him. True love for souls will become in us the spirit of intercession. It is possible to do a lot of faithful and earnest work for others without true love for them. Just as a lawyer or a physician from a love of his or her profession and a high sense of faithfulness to duty may become deeply involved with the needs of clients or patients without any particular love for them. Likewise, servants of Christ may give themselves to their work with devotion and self-sacrificing enthusiasm without any strong Christlike love for souls. It is this lack of love that causes much of our lack of prayer. Only as love of our profession and delight in thoroughness and diligence fall away in the tender compassion of Christ, will love compel us to prayer, because we cannot rest in our work if souls are not saved. True love must pray.

3. *The sense of powerlessness.* We often speak of the power of love. In one sense this is true, and yet the truth has its limitations, which must not be forgotten. The strongest love may be utterly

powerless. A mother might be willing to give her life for her dying child but still not be able to save it. The friend at midnight was most willing to give his guest bread, but he had none. It was this sense of powerlessness, of his inability to help, that sent him begging, "A friend . . . is come to me, and I have nothing to set before him." This sense of powerlessness in God's servants is the very strength of the life of intercession.

"I have nothing to set before him." As this consciousness possesses the minister or missionary, the teacher or worker, intercession becomes the only hope and refuge. I may have knowledge and truth, a loving heart, and the readiness to give myself for those in my charge, but the bread of heaven I cannot give them. For all my love and zeal, "I have nothing to set before them." Blessed is the man who has made the declaration "I have nothing" the motto of his ministry. He thinks of Judgment Day and the danger of souls. He sees what a supernatural power and life is needed to save men from sin. He feels how utterly insufficient he is—all he can do is to meet their physical need. "I have nothing" urges him to pray. As he thinks of the midnight darkness and the hungry souls, intercession appears to him as the only hope, the one thing in which his love can take refuge.

As a warning to all who are strong and wise to work, for the encouragement of all who are weak, remember this truth: The sense of powerlessness is the soul of intercession. The simplest, weakest Christian can pray down blessing from an almighty God.

4. *Faith in prayer.* What the man himself doesn't have, another can supply. He has a rich friend nearby who will be both able and willing to give him what he needs. He is sure that if he only asks, he will receive. This faith makes him leave his home at

midnight; if he himself has no bread to give, he can ask his friend.

We need this simple, confident faith that God will give what we ask. Where faith truly exists, there will be no possibility of our not praying. In God's Word we have everything that can stir and strengthen such faith in us. The heaven our natural eye sees is one great ocean of sunshine, with its light and heat giving beauty and fruitfulness to the earth. In the same manner, Scripture shows us God's true heaven, which is filled with all spiritual blessings—divine light and love and life, heavenly joy and peace and power, all available to us. It shows God waiting, even delighting, to bestow these blessings on us in answer to prayer.

By hundreds of promises and testimonies, Scripture urges us to believe that prayer will be heard, that what we cannot possibly do ourselves for those whom we want to help can be done by prayer. Surely there can be no question as to our believing that our prayer will be heard. We see also that through prayer the poorest and weakest can dispense blessings to the needy, and each of us, even though poor, might make many rich.

5. *Persistence that prevails.* The faith of the host in our story met a sudden and unexpected obstacle—his rich friend refused to hear. "I cannot rise and give to you." The loving heart had not counted on this disappointment. It cannot consent to accept it. The supplicant presses his threefold plea: Here is my needy friend; you have abundance; I am your friend. Then he refuses to accept a denial. The love that opened his house at midnight and provided what was needed must conquer.

Here is the central lesson of the parable. In our intercession we may find that there is difficulty and delay in the answer. It may be as if God says, "I cannot give to you now." It is not easy, against all appearances, to hold firm to our confidence that He will hear, and then to continue to persevere in full assurance that we will have what we ask. Even so, this is what God desires from us. He highly prizes our confidence in Him, which is essentially the highest honor the creature can render the Creator. He will therefore do anything to train us in the exercise of this trust in Him. Blessed is the one who is not staggered by God's delay or silence or apparent refusal, but is strong in faith, giving glory to God. Such faith perseveres, persistently, if need be, and will not fail to inherit the blessing.

6. *Certainty of a rich reward*. "I tell you . . . because of the man's boldness he will get up and give him as much as he needs." Oh, that we might believe in the certainty of an answer! A prophet long ago said, "Let not your hands be weak; *for your work will be rewarded*." If only all who feel it difficult to pray much would fix their eye on the reward, and in faith learn to count upon the divine assurance that their prayer is not in vain.

If we will only believe in God and His faithfulness, intercession will become the first thing we take refuge in when we seek a blessing for others. It will be the very last thing for which we cannot find time. It will also become an act of joy and hope, because while we pray, we recognize that we are sowing seed that will bring forth fruit. Disappointment is impossible: "I tell you . . . he will get up and give him as much as he needs."

Lovers of souls and workers in the service of the Gospel, take courage. Time spent in prayer will yield more than time given to your other work. Prayer alone gives work its worth and its success. Prayer opens the way for God himself to work in us and through us. Let our primary work as God's messengers be intercession; in it, we secure the presence and power of God to go with us.

"Suppose one of you has a friend, and he goes to him at midnight and says, 'Friend, lend me three loaves of bread.'" This friend is none other than our God. In the darkness of midnight, at the most unlikely time and in the greatest need, when we have to say of those we love and care for, "I have nothing to set before them," let us remember that we have a rich Friend in heaven. The everlasting God and Father waits to be asked.

Let us confess before God our lack of prayer. Let us admit that the lack of faith, of which our lack of prayer is the proof, is the symptom of a life that is not spiritual, that is still under the power of self and the flesh and the world. Let us by faith in the Lord Jesus, who told this parable and who waits to make every part of it true in us, give ourselves to be intercessors. Let every glimpse of souls needing help, let every stirring of the Spirit of compassion, let every sense of our own powerlessness to bless, every difficulty in the way of our getting an answer, all combine to urge us to do this one thing: with all boldness to cry to the God who alone can and will help us.

But if we indeed feel that we have failed in a life of intercession until now, let us do our utmost to train a young generation of Christians who will profit from our mistake and avoid it. Moses could not enter the land of Canaan, but there was one thing he could do. He could at God's bidding "commission Joshua, and encourage him and strengthen him" (Deuteronomy 3:28). If it is too late for us to make good our failure, let us at least encourage those who come after us to enter into the good land, the blessed life of unceasing prayer.

The model intercessor is the model Christian layperson. To get from God, and then to give to others what we ourselves receive from day to day, is the secret of successful work. Intercession is the blessed link between our powerlessness and God's omnipotence.

Chapter 4

Because of His Boldness

"I tell you, though he will not get up and give him the bread because he is his friend, yet because of the man's boldness he will get up and give him as much as he needs."

Luke 11:8

Then Jesus told his disciples a parable to show them that they should always pray and not give up. . . . "Listen to what the unjust judge says. And will not God bring about justice for his chosen ones, who cry out to him day and night? Will he keep putting them off? I tell you, he will see that they get justice, and quickly."

Luke 18:1, 6–8

Our Lord Jesus thought it so important for us to know the need of perseverance and boldness in prayer that He gave two parables to teach us this. This is sufficient proof that this aspect of prayer contains prayer's greatest difficulty and its highest power. He would have us know that in prayer all will not be so easy and smooth. We must expect difficulties, which can be conquered only by persistent, determined perseverance.

In the parables, our Lord represents the difficulty as existing on the side of the persons to whom the petition was addressed, that boldness is needed to overcome their reluctance to hear. Between God and us, however, the difficulty is not on His side but on *ours*. In the first parable, He tells us that our Father is more willing to give good things to those who ask Him than any earthly father is to give his child bread. In the second, He assures us that God longs to avenge His chosen ones quickly.

Urgent prayer is not necessary because God has to be made willing or available to bless. Rather, the need lies altogether in us. However, it was not possible to find any earthly illustration of a loving father or a willing friend from whom the needed lesson of boldness could be taught. He therefore uses the *unwilling* friend and the *unjust* judge to encourage in us the faith that perseverance can overcome every obstacle.

The difficulty is not in God's love or power but in us and in our own incapacity to receive the blessing. But because there is this difficulty with us, this lack of spiritual preparedness, there is also a difficulty with God. His wisdom, His righteousness, even His love, dare not give us what would do us harm if we received it too soon or too easily.

The sin, or the consequence of sin, that makes it impossible for God to give at once what we ask is a barrier on God's side as well as ours. The attempt to break through this power of sin in those for whom we pray or in ourselves is what makes the striving and the conflict of prayer such a reality.

Throughout history men have prayed under a sense that there are difficulties in the heavenly world to be overcome. They plead with God for the removal of these unknown obstacles. In that persevering supplication they are brought into a state of utter brokenness and helplessness, of entire resignation to Him, of union with His will, and of faith that can take hold of Him. Then the hindrances in themselves *and* in heaven are both overcome. *As God conquers them, so to speak, they conquer God.* As God prevails over us, we prevail with God.

God has so created us that the more clearly we see the reasonableness of a demand, the more readily we will surrender to it. One great reason for our negligence of prayer is that there appears to be something arbitrary or at least something incomprehensible in the call to such persistent prayer. We need to see that this apparent difficulty is a divine necessity, and that in the very nature of things it is a source of unspeakable blessing. Then we should be ready with glad hearts to give ourselves to continue in prayer. Let us try to understand how the call to boldness and the difficulty it puts in our way is one of our greatest privileges.

Have you ever noticed what a part difficulties play in our everyday life? They bring out our strong traits as nothing else can. They strengthen and ennoble our character. It has even been said that people who live in colder climates tend to be stronger in will and purpose than those who live in milder climes. Warmer climates encourage ease and relaxation.

All nature has been so arranged by God that in sowing and reaping, just as in seeking oil or gold, nothing is found without hard work and effort. What is education but a daily developing and disciplining of the mind by new difficulties that the student must overcome? The moment a lesson has become easy, the student is advanced to one that is higher and more difficult. Collectively and individually, it is in confronting and mastering difficulties that our highest attainments are found.

It is the same in our relationship with God. Imagine what the result would be if the child of God had only to kneel down, ask, receive, and go away. What unspeakable loss to the spiritual life would result. In the very difficulty and delay that calls for persevering prayer, the true blessedness of the spiritual life is found. There we learn how little we delight in fellowship with God and how small our faith is in Him. We discover how earthly and unspiritual our heart is, and how we need God's Holy Spirit. There we are brought to know our own weakness and unworthiness and to yield to God's Spirit to pray through us. There we take our place in Christ Jesus and abide in Him as our only advocate with the Father. There our own will and way are crucified. And there we rise in Christ to newness of life, because now our whole will is dependent upon God and fixed upon His glory. Let us begin to praise God for the need and the difficulty of persistent prayer as one of His choicest means of grace.

Think about what our Lord Jesus owed to the difficulties in His path. In Gethsemane it was as if the Father would not hear Him. He prayed even more earnestly until he *was* heard. In the path He opened up for us, He learned obedience by the things He suffered and thus was made perfect. His will was given up to God. His faith in God was proven and strengthened. The prince of this world, with all his temptation, was overcome. This is the new and living way He consecrated for us. It is in persevering prayer that we walk with and are made partakers of His very Spirit. Prayer is a form of crucifixion; it is our fellowship with Christ's cross, our giving over of our flesh to death.

We should be ashamed of our reluctance to sacrifice our flesh, our will, and the world. Such resistance leads to a reluctance to pray. Nature itself and Christ teach that the difficulty of persistence in prayer is our highest privilege. Overcoming the difficulties brings the richest blessings.

Importunity, or persistence, has various elements. The primary ones are perseverance, determination, and intensity. Importunity begins with the refusal to readily accept a denial. This refusal develops into a determination to persevere, to spare no time or trouble, until an answer comes. Then this determination grows into an intensity in which the whole being is given to God in supplication. Boldness lays hold of God's strength. At one time it is quiet and restful, at another passionate and bold. At one point it waits in patience, at another it claims at once what it desires. In whatever form, importunity insists, *God hears prayer; I must be heard.*

Remember the wonderful examples we have of persistence in the Old Testament saints. Think of Abraham as he pleads for Sodom. Time after time he renews his prayer, until the sixth time he has to say, "Let not the Lord be angry." He does not cease until he knows God's condescension, each time consenting to his petition, until he has learned how far he can go, that he has entered into God's mind, and that he has rested in God's will. For Abraham's sake Lot was saved: "God remembered Abraham, and sent Lot out of the midst of the overthrow." Shouldn't we who have redemption and promises for the lost— which Abraham never knew—begin to plead more earnestly with God on their behalf?

Think of Jacob when he feared to meet Esau. The angel of the Lord met him in the dark and wrestled with him. When the angel saw that he did not prevail, he said, "Let me go." Jacob said, "I will not let you go." So the angel blessed him there. That boldness that declared "I will not," and forced from the reluctant angel the blessing, so pleased God that a new name was given to Jacob: Israel—he who strives with God—"for you have striven with God and with men and have prevailed."

Through the ages God's children have sought to understand what these parables and stories teach: God holds himself back from us until what is of the flesh and self and laziness in us is overcome. Then we can prevail with Him so that He *can* and *must* bless us.

Why is it that so many have no desire for the honor of being princes of God, strivers with God, and prevailing pray-ers? What our Lord taught us—"Whatever you ask for in prayer, *believe that you have received it, and it will be yours*" (Mark 11:24)—is nothing more than His expression of Jacob's words, "I will not let you go until you bless me." This is the persistence He teaches. We must learn to claim and receive the blessing.

Remember Moses' words when Israel made the golden calf: "Moses went back to the LORD and said, 'Oh, what a great sin these people have committed! They have made themselves gods of gold. But now, please forgive their sin—but if not, then blot me out of the book you have written' " (Exodus 32:31–32). That was importunity. Moses would rather have died than not have his people with him.

When God heard him and said He would send His angel with the people, Moses came again. He would not be content until in answer to his prayer God himself would go with them (33:12, 17–18); God had said, "I will do the very thing you have asked." After that, in answer to Moses' prayer, "Now show me your glory," God made His goodness pass before him. Then Moses at once began pleading, " 'O Lord, if I have found favor in your eyes . . . then let the Lord go with us' " (34:9). And "Moses was there with the LORD forty days and forty nights" (34:28).

As an intercessor, Moses used importunity with God and prevailed. He proves that the one who truly lives near to God, and with whom God speaks face-to-face, partakes of that same power of intercession that there is in Jesus, who is at God's right hand and ever lives to pray for us.

Elijah is another example of persistent prayer: first for fire and then for rain. In the former, his importunity claims and receives an immediate answer. In the latter, he bows himself down to the earth, his face between his knees. His answer to the servant who had gone to look toward the sea and come with the message "There is nothing," was "Go again seven times." Here was the boldness of perseverance. Elijah had told Ahab there would be rain. He knew it was coming. Still he prayed until the seven times were fulfilled.

It is of Elijah and this prayer that James teaches, "Pray for each other. . . . The prayer of a righteous man is powerful and effective. Elijah was a man just like us" (5:16–17). Some will feel constrained to cry out, "Where is the Lord God of Elijah?"—this God who draws forth such effectual prayer, and hears it so wonderfully. His name should be praised. He still waits to be inquired of! Faith in a prayer-hearing God will make a prayer-loving Christian.

Remember the marks of the true intercessor as taught in the parable: (1) a sense of the need of souls; (2) a Christlike love in the heart; (3) a consciousness of personal powerlessness; (4) faith in the power of prayer; (5) courage to persevere in spite of refusal; (6) and the assurance of an abundant reward. These are the qualities that change a Christian into an intercessor and call forth the power of prevailing prayer.

These are the elements that mark the Christian life with beauty and health. They equip a man for being a blessing in the world and make him a true Christian minister, one who obtains from God the bread of heaven to dispense to the hungry. These are the attitudes that call forth the highest heroic virtues of the life of faith.

There is nothing to which the nobility of natural character owes more than the spirit of enterprise and daring that *battles* with difficulties in travel or war, in politics or science, and *conquers*. No labor or expense for the sake of victory is begrudged. So should we who are Christians be able to face the difficulties that we meet in prayer. As we "labor" and "strive" in prayer, our renewed will asserts its royal right to claim in the name of Christ what it desires, and wields its God-given power in influencing the destinies of people.

Those of this world sacrifice ease and pleasure in their entrepreneurial pursuits. Will we as Christians be cowardly and complacent in fighting our way through to the place where we can find liberty for the captive and salvation for the lost? Let each servant of Christ learn to know his high calling. The Spirit of the King ever lives in us to pray. It is from heaven that the blessings the world needs must be released through persevering, bold, and believing prayer. The Holy Spirit, in answer to fervent prayer, will take possession of us and do His work through us.

Let us acknowledge how vain our work for God has been due to our lack of prayer. Let us change our methods and make continuing, persistent prayer the proof that we look to God for all things and that we believe that He hears us and answers us.

Chapter 5

The Life That Can Pray

"If you remain in me and my words remain in you, ask whatever you wish, and it will be given you."

John 15:7

The prayer of a righteous man is powerful and effective.

James 5:16

Dear friends, if our hearts do not condemn us, we have confidence before God and receive from him anything we ask, because we obey his commands and do what pleases him.

1 John 3:21–22

Here on earth, the influence of one who asks a favor for someone else depends entirely on his character and the relationship he has to him with whom he is interceding. *It is who he is that gives weight to what he asks.* It is no different with God. Our power in prayer depends upon our life. When our life is right, we will know how to pray so as to please God, and prayer will secure the answer.

The texts quoted above all point in this direction. "If you remain in me," our Lord says, "ask whatever you wish, and it will be given you." According to James, it is the prayer of "a righteous man" that "is powerful and effective." We receive "whatsoever we ask," John says, "*because* we keep his commandments."

A lack of power to pray aright and with perseverance—in fact, any lack of power in prayer with God—points to some lack in the Christian life. Only as we learn to live the life that pleases God will He be able to give us what we ask.

Let us learn from our Lord Jesus, in the parable of the vine, what the healthy, vigorous life is that asks and receives whatever it wishes. He says, "If you remain in me and my words remain in you, ask whatever you wish, and it will be given you." He says at the close of the parable, "You did not choose me, but I chose you and appointed you to go and bear fruit—fruit that will last. Then the Father will give you whatever you ask in my name" (John 15:7, 16).

What, according to the parable, is the life that one must lead in order to bear fruit and then to ask and receive what it wishes? What must we be or do to enable us to pray as we should and to receive what we ask? The answer is in one word: *branch*. We are branches of Christ, the Living Vine. We must simply live like branches and abide in Christ; then we can ask what we wish and it will be done for us.

We all know what a branch is and what its essential characteristic is. It is simply a growth off the vine, produced by it and appointed to bear fruit. It has only one purpose: It is there at the bidding of the vine that through it the vine might bear and ripen its precious fruit. Just as the vine solely and wholly lives to produce the sap that makes the grape, so the branch has no other aim and object but to receive that sap and bear the grape. Its only work is to serve the vine that through it the vine may do its work.

Is it not clear that the believer, the branch of Christ, the Heavenly Vine, is just as literally and exclusively to live only so that Christ may bear fruit through him? Is it meant that a true Christian as a branch is to be just as absorbed in and devoted to the work of bearing fruit to the glory of God as Christ the Vine was on earth and now is in heaven? This and nothing less is what is meant. It is to such a person that the unlimited prayer promises of the parable are given.

It is the branch-life existing solely for the Vine that will have the power to pray aright. As we are abiding in Him, and His words are abiding and ruling in our heart and life—transmitted into our very being—there will be grace to pray and faith to receive "whatever we wish."

Let us join the two concepts and take them both in their simple, literal form as well as their infinite, divine grandeur. The promises of our Lord's farewell discourse, with their sixfold repetition of the unlimited—*whatever, anything* (John 14:13–14; 15:7, 16; 16:23–24)—appear to us too large to be taken literally. Therefore, we rationalize them to meet our human ideas of what it appears they ought to be. We separate them from that life of absolute and unlimited devotion to Christ's service for which they were given.

God's covenant is always *give all and take all*. He that is willing to be wholly a branch and nothing but a branch, who is ready to place himself absolutely at the disposal of Jesus, the Vine of God, to bear His fruit through him, and to live every moment only for Him, will receive a divine liberty to claim Christ's *whatever* in all its fullness and a divine wisdom and humility to use it properly.

Such a person will live and pray and claim the Father's promises, even as Christ did, only for God's glory in the salvation of men. He will use his boldness in prayer only with a view to power in intercession and obtaining blessing for others. The unlimited devotion of the branch-life to fruit-bearing and the unlimited access to the treasures of the Vine-life are inseparable. It is the life abiding wholly in Christ that can pray the effective prayer in the name of Christ.

Think for a moment of the men of prayer in Scripture and see in them what kind of life could pray in such power. We spoke of Abraham as an intercessor. What gave him such boldness? He knew that God had chosen and called him away from his home and people to walk before Him so that all nations might be blessed through him. He knew that he had obeyed and forsaken all for God. Implicit obedience, to the very sacrifice of his son, was the law of his life. He did what God asked so that he dared trust God to do what he asked.

We spoke of Moses also as an intercessor. He too had forsaken all for God, "esteeming the reproach of Christ greater riches than the treasures of Egypt." He lived at God's disposal: "As a servant he was faithful in all his house." How often it is written of him, "According to all that the Lord commanded Moses, so he did." No wonder he was so very bold. His heart was right with God. He knew God would hear him. This is no less true of Elijah, the man who stood up to plead for the Lord God of Israel. The man who is ready to risk all for God can count upon God to do all for him.

Men pray only as they live. It is the life that prays. The life that with wholehearted devotion gives up all for God and to God can also claim all from God. Our God longs to prove himself the faithful God and mighty helper of His people. He only waits for hearts wholly turned from the world to himself and open to receive His gifts. The man who loses all will find all and will dare to ask and to receive it.

The branch that truly abides in Christ, the Heavenly Vine, is entirely given up like Christ to bear fruit unto salvation. Christ's words become part of his life so that he may dare ask whatever he wishes—and it will be done.

Where we have not yet attained to that full devotion to which our Lord's disciples were trained, and cannot equal them in their power in prayer, we may, nevertheless, take courage in one fact. Even in the beginning stages of the Christian life, every new step onward in the pursuit of the perfect branch life, and every surrender to live for others through intercessory prayer, will be met by a corresponding liberty to draw near with greater boldness and to expect more frequent answers. The more we pray and the more conscious we become of our inability to pray in power, the more we shall be urged and helped to press on toward the secret of power in prayer—a life that abides in Christ, entirely at His disposal.

If there are those who are asking, in despair of attainment, what the reason is for failure in this blessed branch-life—so simple and yet so mighty—and how they can attain it, let me point them to one of the most precious lessons of the parable of the

Vine. It is one that is often neglected. Jesus said, "I am the true vine, and my Father is the Vinedresser." We have not only Jesus himself, the glorified Son of God, in His divine fullness and out of whose fullness of life and grace we can draw, but there is something more. We have the Father, as the Vinedresser, watching over our abiding in the Vine, seeing to our growth and fruit-bearing. It is not left to our faith or faithfulness to maintain our union with Christ. God, the Father of Christ, who united us with Him, will see to it that the branch is what it should be. He will enable us to bring forth the fruit we were appointed to bear. Hear what Christ said of this: "Every branch that does bear fruit he prunes so that it will be even more fruitful" (John 15:2). More fruit is what the Father seeks; more fruit is what the Father himself will provide. It is for this reason that He, as the Vinedresser, prunes the branches.

Consider what this means: It is said that of all fruit-bearing plants on earth, there is none that produces fruit so full of spirit and from which spirit can be so abundantly distilled as the grapevine. And of all fruit-bearing plants there is none that is so prone to produce wildwood and for which pruning is so indispensable. The one great work that a vinedresser has to do for the branch every year is to prune it. Other plants can for a time do without it and still bear fruit; the grapevine *must* have it. So the branch that desires to abide in Christ and bring forth much fruit and be able to ask whatsoever it wishes, must do one thing: It must trust in and yield itself to this divine cleansing and pruning.

What does the vinedresser cut away with his pruning knife? He cuts the wood that the branch has produced—true, honest wood with the true vine nature in it.

Why must this be cut away? Because it draws away the strength and life of the vine and hinders the flow of the juice to the fruit. The more it is cut back, the less wood there is in the branch, and the more all the sap can go to the grape. The wood of the branch must decrease that the fruit for the vine may increase. In obedience to the law of all nature, death is the way to life, gain comes through sacrifice, the rich and luxuriant growth of wood must be cut off and cast away that the more abundant life may be seen in the cluster of fruit.

In the same way, child of God, branch of the Heavenly Vine, there is in you that which appears perfectly innocent and legitimate but which saps away your interest and strength. It must be pruned and cleansed. We saw what power in prayer men like Abraham, Moses, and Elijah had, and we know what fruit they bore. But we also know what it cost them. God had to separate them from their surroundings over and over to draw them away from any trust in themselves, so they would seek their life in Him alone.

It is only as our own will, our strength, our effort, our pleasure, are cut back—even where these appear perfectly natural and sinless—that the whole energies of our being are free and open to receive the vital life of the Heavenly Vine, the Holy Spirit. Then we shall bear much fruit. It is in the surrender of what by nature we hold onto but yield to God's holy pruning knife that we shall come to what Christ chose and appointed us for—to bear fruit, that whatever we ask the Father in Christ's name, He may give us.

Christ tells us what the pruning knife is in the next verse: "You are already clean because of the word I have spoken to you."

As He says later, "Sanctify them by the truth; your word is truth" (John 17:17). "For the word of God is living and active. Sharper than any double-edged sword, it penetrates even to dividing soul and spirit, joints and marrow; it judges the thoughts and attitudes of the heart" (Hebrews 4:12).

Christ had spoken to His disciples heart-searching words on love and humility, on being the least, and, like himself, the servant of all, on denying self, and taking up the cross, and losing their life. Through His Word, the Father had cleansed them, cut away all confidence in themselves or the world, and prepared them for the inflowing and filling of the Spirit of the Heavenly Vine. We cannot cleanse ourselves. God the Father is the Vinedresser. We may confidently entrust ourselves to His care.

Beloved brethren—ministers, missionaries, teachers, layworkers, believers old and young—are you mourning your lack of prayer and the resultant lack of power in prayer? Come and listen to your beloved Lord as He tells you, *Only be a branch. Unite yourself to and identify yourself with the Heavenly Vine, and your prayers will be effective.*

Are you grieving because your problem is that you do not or cannot live this branch-life, abiding in Him? "More fruit" is not only your desire but the Father's also. He is the Vinedresser, who cleanses the fruitful branch that it may bear more fruit.

Cast yourself upon God to do in you what is impossible to do for yourself. Count upon a divine cleansing to cut down and take away all the self-confidence and self-effort that has been the cause of your failure. The God who gave you His beloved Son as the Vine, who made you His branch, will He not do His work of pruning to make you fruitful in every good thing, and in prayer and intercession too?

Here is the one who can pray: a branch entirely committed to the Vine and its aims with all responsibility for its pruning cast on the Vinedresser; a branch that is abiding in Christ will bear much fruit. In the power of such a life we will love prayer, we will know *how* to pray, and we will receive whatever we ask.

Chapter 6

Is Prayerlessness Sin?

"You . . . hinder devotion to God."

Job 15:4

"Who is the Almighty, that we should serve him?
What would we gain by praying to him?"

Job 21:15

"Far be it from me that I should sin against the LORD
by failing to pray for you."

1 Samuel 12:23

"I will not be with you anymore unless you destroy whatever
among you is devoted to destruction."

Joshua 7:12

Any deep quickening of the spiritual life of the church will always be accompanied by a deeper sense of sin. This will not begin with theology, which can only describe what God works in the life of His people. Nor does it mean that this deeper sense of sin will be seen only in stronger expressions of self-reproach or penitence (that sometimes indicates a harboring of sin and unbelief as to deliverance).

The true sense of the awfulness of sin and the distain of it will be proven by the intensity of desire for deliverance and the struggle to know what God can do to save us from it—a holy jealousy that desires to sin against God in nothing.

If we are to deal effectively with the lack of prayer in our lives, we must first ask ourselves, "Is prayerlessness sin?" If it is, then how can it be dealt with—discovered, confessed, cast out, and cleansed away?

Jesus is our Savior from sin. Only as we know what sin is can we know the power that saves from sin. The life that can pray effectively is the life of the cleansed branch—the life that knows deliverance from the power of self. To see that our prayerlessness is sin is the first step toward a true and divine deliverance.

The story of Achan has one of the strongest proofs in Scripture that sin robs God's people of His blessing and that God will not tolerate it. At the same time it gives the clearest indication of the principles under which God deals with sin and removes it. In light of the story, let us see if we can learn how to look at the sin of prayerlessness and at the sinfulness that lies at its root. The words "I will not be with you anymore unless you destroy whatever among you is devoted to destruction" take us into the very heart of the story. They suggest a series of priceless lessons around the truth they express, that the presence of sin makes the presence of God impossible.

1. *The presence of God is the great privilege of God's people and their only power against the Enemy.* God promised to Moses, "I

will bring you unto the land." Moses proved that he understood this when God, after the sin of the worship of the golden calf, spoke of withdrawing His presence and sending an angel. Moses refused to accept anything less than God's presence. "How will anyone know that you are pleased with me and with your people unless you go with us? What else will distinguish me and your people from all the other people on the face of the earth?" (Exodus 33:16).

This gave Caleb and Joshua their confidence: The Lord is with us. This gave Israel their victory over Jericho: the presence of God. This is throughout Scripture the great central promise: *I am with you.* This separates the wholehearted believer from the unbeliever and the worldly Christian. The wholehearted believer lives consciously hidden in the secret of God's presence.

2. *Defeat and failure are always due to the loss of God's presence.* This was true at Ai. God had brought His people into Canaan with the promise to give them the land. When the defeat at Ai took place, Joshua felt at once that the cause must be in the withdrawal of God's power. God had not fought for them. His presence had been withheld.

In the Christian life and the work of the church, defeat is always a sign of the loss of God's presence. If we apply this to failure in our prayer life, which leads to failure in our work for God, we will see that all is simply due to our not standing in clear and full fellowship with God. His nearness, His immediate presence, has not been the primary thing sought after and trusted in. He could not work in us as He would like to. Loss of blessing and power is always caused by the loss of God's presence.

3. *The loss of God's presence is always due to some hidden sin.*

Just as pain is nature's warning of some hidden evil in the physical system, defeat is God's voice telling us there is something wrong in the spiritual life. He has given himself wholly to His people. He delights in being with them and revealing to them His love and power. Therefore, He never withdraws himself unless they compel Him to do so by sinning.

Throughout the church there is a sense of defeat. The church has so little power over the masses, educated or otherwise. Powerful conversions are comparatively rare. The lack of holy, consecrated, spiritual Christians devoted to the service of God and their neighbors is felt everywhere. The power of the church for the preaching of the Gospel to the lost is paralyzed by a scarcity of money and of willing workers. This is due to the lack of effective prayer that brings the Holy Spirit in power on the clergy, layworkers, worshipers, missionaries, and finally the lost. Can we deny that the lack of prayer is the sin that prevents God's presence and power from being manifested among us?

4. *God himself will reveal our hidden sin.* We may think we know what the sin is, but only God can reveal its deeper meaning. When He spoke to Joshua, before naming the sin of Achan, God said, "They have violated my covenant, which I commanded them to keep" (Joshua 7:11). God had commanded that all the booty of Jericho, the gold and silver and all that was in it, was to be consecrated unto the Lord and was to come into His treasury. Israel had broken this consecration vow. It had not given God His due. It had robbed God.

What we need is a revelation from God that our lack of prayer is an indication of unfaithfulness to our vow of consecration that gave God all our heart and life. We must see that prayerlessness, with the excuses we make for it, is a greater sin than we thought. It means that we have little taste or desire for fellowship with God. It shows that our faith rests more on our own work and efforts than on the power of God. It shows we have little sense of the heavenly blessing God waits to shower upon us. It means we are not ready to sacrifice the ease and confidence of the flesh for persistent pleading before God. It shows that the spirituality of our life and our abiding in Christ is too weak to allow us to prevail in prayer.

When the pressure of work for Christ becomes the excuse for our not finding time to seek and secure His presence and power, it proves we have no proper sense of our absolute dependence upon God. There is obviously no grasp of the divine work of God in which we are only His instruments. Neither is there a sense of mission or full surrender to Christ Jesus himself.

If we were to yield to God's Spirit to show us that this reveals a neglect of prayer and of our allowing other things to crowd it out, all our excuses would fall away. We would prostrate ourselves before Him and cry, "We have sinned! We have sinned!" Samuel once said, "As for me, God forbid that I should sin against the Lord in ceasing to pray for you." *Ceasing from prayer is sin against God.*

5. *When God discloses sin, it must be confessed and forsaken.* When the defeat at Ai came, Joshua and Israel were ignorant of the cause. God dealt with Israel as a nation, as one body, and the sin of one member was visited on all. Israel as a whole was ignorant of the sin but still suffered for it. The church may be ignorant of the greatness of their sin of prayerlessness. Individuals may never have looked upon it as actual transgression. Even so,

the punishment it brings is sure and certain.

But when the sin is no longer hidden, when the Holy Spirit begins to convict, then comes the needed heart-searching. In our story, the combination of individual and corporate responsibility is very serious. In the expression "tribe by tribe" and "family by family," each person felt himself under the eye of God. And when Achan was taken, he had to make his confession. In the corporate aspect, we see all of Israel first suffering and then being dealt with by God. Then Achan and his family, with all of his possessions, along with the stolen goods, are taken away and destroyed.

If we have reason to believe prayerlessness is the sin that is in our camp, let us begin with personal and united confession. Then let us come before God to put away the sin and destroy it. At the very threshold of Israel's history in Canaan, this heap of stones stands in the valley of Achor to tell us that God cannot tolerate sin, that God will not dwell where sin is present, and that *if we really want God's presence in power, sin must be put away from us.*

Let us look squarely at the facts. There may be other sins, but not praying as Christ and Scripture teach us is certainly one that causes the loss of God's presence. Let us uncover it before God and give it up. Let us yield ourselves to God and obey His voice. Let no fear of past failure, no threatening array of temptations or duties or excuses keep us back. It is a simple question of obedience. Are we going to give ourselves over to God and His Spirit to live a life of prayer that is well-pleasing to Him or not?

If it is God who has been withholding His presence, exposing the sin, calling for its destruction and a return to obedience, surely we can count upon His grace to strengthen us for the life He asks of us. It is not a question of what you can do. It is a question of whether you will with your whole heart give God what is due Him and allow His will to be done in your life.

6. *When sin is cast out, God's presence is restored.* From this day forward there is not a word in the book of Joshua about defeat in battle. The story shows the Israelites going on from victory to victory. God's presence gives power to overcome every enemy.

This truth is so simple that the very ease with which we agree to it robs it of its power. Let us stop and think what it implies. God's presence restored means victory secured. Then if there is defeat, we are responsible for it. Some sin, somewhere, must be causing it. We need to discover the sin and put it away. The moment the sin is put away, we may expect God's presence to return. Surely all of us are under solemn obligation to search our life and see if we are guilty of the neglect of prayer or if some other sin is causing us to lose fellowship.

God never speaks to His people of sin except with a view to saving them from it. *The same light that reveals the sin will show the way out of it.* The same power that condemns sin, if humbly yielded to, will give us the power to rise up and conquer.

It is God who is speaking to His church and to us: "He saw that there was no one, he was appalled that there was no one to intervene" (Isaiah 59:16). He sought for someone to stand in the gap and found none. The God who speaks like this is the same who will work the change in His children. He will make the "valley of Achor" a door of hope.

Let us not be afraid, and let us not cling to the excuses and explanations that circumstances suggest. But rather let us confess, "We have sinned; we are sinning; we dare not sin any longer."

In this matter of prayer, God does not demand of us impossibilities. He does not weary us with an impractical ideal. He asks us to pray no more than He gives enabling grace. He will always give the strength to do what He asks; our intercession will, day by day, be a pleasure to Him, and to us—a source of strength to our work, and a channel of blessing to those for whom we pray.

God dealt personally with Joshua, with Israel, and with Achan. We must allow Him to deal personally with us concerning the sin of prayerlessness, its consequences in our life and work, and concerning our deliverance from sin.

Wait in stillness before God until He overshadows you with His presence. Wait until He leads you out of your argument as to human possibilities, where conviction of sin can never be deep and full deliverance can never come. Be still before God in a time of quietness, so that He may deal with the matter at hand. He will not rest until He has finished His work. Leave yourself in God's hands.

Chapter 7

Who Shall Deliver Us?

"Is there no balm in Gilead? Is there no physician there? Why then is there no healing for the wound of my people?"

Jeremiah 8:22

"Return, faithless people; I will cure you of backsliding. Yes, we will come to you, for you are the LORD our God."

Jeremiah 3:22

Heal me, O LORD, and I will be healed; save me and I will be saved, for you are the one I praise.

Jeremiah 17:14

What a wretched man I am! Who will rescue me from this body of death? Thanks be to God—through Jesus Christ our Lord! Through Christ Jesus the law of the Spirit of life set me free from the law of sin and death.

Romans 7:24–25; 8:2

During one of our conventions a gentleman called upon me for advice and help. He was obviously an earnest Christian and well-educated man. For some years he had been in extremely difficult surroundings, trying to witness for Christ. The result was a sense of failure and unhappiness. His complaint was that he had no desire for the Word, or joy in it, and that though he prayed, his heart was not in it. If he spoke to others or gave a gospel tract, it was under a sense of obligation. Love and joy were not present in his service for God. He longed to be filled with the Spirit, but the more he sought it, the further away the Spirit seemed to be. What was he to think of his situation? Was there any way out of it?

My answer was that the whole matter appeared to me very simple. He was living under the law and not under grace. As long as he did so, there could be no change. He listened attentively but could not understand what I meant.

I pointed out the distinct contrasts between law and grace. Law demands. Grace bestows. Law commands but gives no strength to obey. Grace promises and performs, doing all we need to do. Law burdens and casts down and condemns. Grace comforts and makes strong and glad. Law appeals to self to do its utmost. Grace points to Christ to do all things. Law calls forth effort and strain and urges us toward a goal we can never reach. Grace works in us all of God's blessed will.

I explained to the man that rather than striving against all this failure, he should first acknowledge it fully and then face the reality of his own powerlessness just as God had been trying to show him. With his confession of failure and lack of power, he should fall down before God in utter helplessness. There he would learn that unless grace delivered him and gave him strength, he could never do better than he had been doing. But grace would indeed work all that was needed for him. He must come out from under the law and self-effort and take his place under grace.

Later he told me the diagnosis had been correct; he admitted that submitting to grace was the answer. But still, so deep was the thought that he must *do something*—that he must by his faithfulness help to receive the work of grace—in reality he feared his life would not be very different. He thought that he would not be equal to the strain of new difficulties that were cropping up. In the midst of a seeming earnestness to find his way, I sensed that an undertone of despair reigned; he was certain he could not live in the way he knew he ought to.

I have noticed this tone of hopelessness before. Every minister who has come into close contact with souls who are seeking to live wholly for God, to "walk worthy of the Lord unto all well pleasing," knows that this makes true progress impossible. When we speak of a lack of prayer and the desire to live a fuller prayer life, there are many difficulties to be faced! We have so often resolved to pray more and better, and have utterly failed.

We don't always have the strength of will that some have, so that with one resolve we can turn around and change our habits. The pressure of our daily responsibilities is as great as it has ever been; it is as difficult as ever to find time for more prayer. And we do not all have real enjoyment in prayer, which would enable us to persevere. We do not possess the power to plead with God in intercession as we know we should. Our prayers, instead of being full of joy and strength, are often a source of self-condemnation and doubt. We have at times mourned and confessed our prayerlessness and resolved to do better; but we do not expect an answer, for we see no way for any great change to take place.

As long as this spirit prevails, there can be very little hope of improvement. Discouragement brings defeat. One of the first objectives of a good physician is to awaken hope in his patient; without it, he knows medication could profit little. No teaching from God's Word as to the responsibility, the urgency, or the privilege of more and effective prayer will avail while in our heads we listen to the lie: *There is no hope.*

Our first purpose here is to find out the hidden cause of our failure and despair, and then to give divine assurance of deliverance. Unless we are to sit back and accept our situation, we must listen to and join in the question, "Is there no balm in Gilead? Is there no physician there? Why then is there no healing for the wound of my people?" We must listen and receive into our heart the divine promise: " 'Return, faithless Israel . . . I will frown on you no longer, for I am merciful . . . I will not be angry forever' " (Jeremiah 3:12).

We must come with our personal prayers and with faith that there will be personal answers. We must even begin to claim an answer to our lack of prayer and believe that God will help us: "Heal me, O LORD, and I will be healed" (Jeremiah 17:14).

It is always important to distinguish between the symptoms of a disease and the disease itself. Weakness and failure in prayer is a sign of weakness in the spiritual life. If a patient were to ask a doctor to give him something to stimulate his weak pulse, he would be told that this is not the issue. The pulse is the index of the state of the heart and the whole system. The doctor strives to have health restored, but he must first determine the cause of the weak pulse.

Everyone who wants to pray more faithfully and effectively

must learn that his whole spiritual life is likely in a sickly state and needs restoration. As he looks not only at his shortcomings in prayer but at his lack in the life of faith, of which this is a symptom, he will become fully aware of the serious nature of the disease. He will then see the need of a radical change in his whole life and walk, if his prayer life—which is simply the pulse of the spiritual system—is to indicate health and vitality.

God has so created us that the exercise of every healthy function causes joy. Prayer is meant to be as simple and natural as breathing or working is to a healthy person. The reluctance we feel and the failure we confess are God's reminders to acknowledge our disease and to come to Him for the healing He has promised.

What is the disease of which a lack of prayer is a symptom? We cannot find a better answer than the words "You are not under the law but under grace."

We have suggested the possibility of two types of Christian life. There may be a life partly under the law and partly under grace; or a life entirely under grace, free of self-effort and experiencing divine strength. In other words, a true believer might still be living partly under the law, in the power of self-effort, striving to do what he cannot accomplish. The continued failure in his Christian life he admits is due to one thing: *He trusts in himself and tries to do his best.* He does, indeed, pray and look to God for help, but it is still *he* who does the work.

In the epistles to the Romans, Corinthians, and Galatians, Paul tells believers that they have not received the spirit of bondage again, that they are free from the law, that they are no more servants but sons. He warns them to beware of becoming entangled again with the yoke of bondage. He continually draws the contrast between the law and grace, between the flesh, which is under the law, and the Spirit, who is the gift of grace, and through whom grace does all its work.

In our day, just as in the days of the early church, the great danger is living under the law and serving God in the strength of the flesh. With the great majority of Christians, it appears to be the state in which they remain all their lives. This explains the tremendous lack of true holy living and power in prayer. They do not know that all failure can have but one cause: *We seek to do ourselves what grace alone can do in us*—and what grace most certainly will do.

Many will not be prepared to admit that their problem is that they are not living "under grace." Impossible, they say. "From the depth of my heart," a Christian cries, "I believe and know that there is no good in me, and that I owe everything to grace alone." A minister claims, "I have spent my life and found my glory in preaching and exalting the doctrines of free grace." A missionary declares, "How could I ever have thought of seeing the heathen saved if my only confidence had not been in the message I brought and the power I trusted of God's abounding grace?" Surely it cannot be said that our failures in prayer—and we sadly confess them—are owed to our not living under grace. This cannot be the problem.

We know how often a person may be suffering from a disease without knowing it. What he counts a slight ailment turns out to be a severe problem. Do not be too sure that you are not still largely living "under the law," while considering yourselves to be living wholly "under grace."

Very frequently the reason for this mistake is the limited meaning attached to the word *grace*. Just as we limit God himself by our small or unbelieving thoughts of Him, so we limit His grace at the very moment that we are delighting in terms like the "riches of grace" and "grace exceedingly abundant." From John Bunyan's *Pilgrim's Progress* onward, has not the very term "grace abounding" been confined to the one great truth of free justification with ever-renewed pardon and eternal glory for the vilest of sinners, while the other equally blessed truth of "grace abounding" in sanctification is not fully known?

Paul writes, "Much more those who receive abundance of grace ... will reign in life through Jesus Christ" (Romans 5:17 NKJV). That reigning in life, as conqueror over sin, is for here on earth. "Where sin abounded" in the heart and life, "grace did much more abound ... even so might grace reign through righteousness" in the whole life and being of the believer. It is about this reign of grace in the soul that Paul asks, "Shall we continue in sin, that grace may abound?" and answers, "God forbid!" (Romans 5:20–21; 6:1–2).

Grace is not only pardon *of* but power *over* sin; grace takes the place sin had in a life. Grace undertakes—just as sin reigned within in the power of death—to reign in the power of Christ's life. It is of this grace that Christ spoke, "My grace is sufficient for you" (2 Corinthians 12:8). Paul answered, "[I will] glory in my infirmities ... for, when I am weak, then am I strong" (2 Corinthians 12:9–10 KJV). When we are willing to confess ourselves utterly powerless and helpless, His grace comes in to work all in us, as Paul elsewhere teaches, "God is able to make *all grace* abound toward you; that ye, *always* having *all suffi-*

ciency in *all things,* may abound to *every good work*" (2 Timothy 2:21 KJV).

Often a seeker after God and salvation has read his Bible for a long time and still has never seen the truth of a free and full and immediate justification by faith. When once his eyes were opened, and he accepted it, he was amazed to find it everywhere. Even many believers, who hold the doctrines of free grace as applied to pardon, have never seen its wondrous meaning. It undertakes to work our whole life in us, and *actually give us strength every moment* for whatever the Father would have us be and do. When God's light shines into our heart with this blessed truth, then we understand Paul's words "Not I, but the grace of God." There again you have the twofold Christian life. The one in which "not I"—I am nothing, I can do nothing—has not yet become a reality and the other, when the wondrous exchange has been made and grace has taken the place of our effort. Then we say and know, "I live; yet not I, but Christ lives in me." It may then become a lifelong experience. "The grace of our Lord was exceeding abundant with faith and love, which is in Christ Jesus" (1 Timothy 1:14 KJV).

Do you think it is possible that this has been lacking in your life, has been the cause of your failure in prayer? You knew not how grace would enable you to pray when once your whole life was under its power. You sought by earnest effort to conquer your reluctance or deadness in prayer but failed. By shame or love you tried to overcome your failure, but they did not help. Is it not worthwhile to ask the Lord whether the message I bring you may not be truer for you than you think?

Your lack of prayer is due to a stagnant state of life. The condition is nothing but this: You have not accepted for daily life and responsibility the full salvation the Word brings: "You are not under the law but under grace." As universal and deep-reaching as the demand of the law and the reign of sin, is the provision of grace and the power by which it makes us reign in life.

Paul wrote, "For sin shall not be your master, because you are not under law, but under grace," and in the chapter that follows he gives us a picture of a believer's life under the law. This life ends with the bitter experience, "What a wretched man I am! Who will rescue me from this body of death?" His answer, "I thank God through Jesus Christ our Lord," shows there is deliverance from a life held captive under sinful habits that we have struggled against in vain.

Deliverance is through the Holy Spirit giving the full experience of what the life of Christ can work in us: "The law of the Spirit of life set me free from the law of sin and death." The law of God could only deliver us into the power of the law of sin and death. The grace of God can bring us into and keep us in the liberty of the Spirit. We can be made free from the sad life under the power that led us captive so that we did what we did not wish to do. The Spirit of life in Christ can free us from our continual failure in prayer and enable us in this, too, to walk worthy of the Lord unto all well-pleasing.

Do not despair or lose hope, because there is a solution. There is a Physician. There is healing for our sickness. What is impossible with man is possible with God. What you see no possibility of doing, grace will do. Confess your sickness. Trust the Physician. Claim the healing. Pray the prayer of faith: "Heal me, O LORD, and I will be healed." You too can become a person of prayer and pray the effective prayer that avails.

Note: I ought to say, for the encouragement of all, that the gentleman, of whom I spoke earlier in this chapter, at a convention two weeks later, saw and claimed the rest of faith in trusting God for all. A letter from him tells me he has found that His grace is sufficient.

Chapter 8

Will You Be Made Whole?

When Jesus saw him lying there and learned that he had been in this
condition for a long time, he asked him, "Do you want to get well?" "Sir,"
the invalid replied, "I have no one to help me into the pool when the
water is stirred. While I am trying to get in, someone else goes down
ahead of me." Then Jesus said to him, "Get up! Pick up your mat and
walk." At once the man was cured; he picked up his mat and walked.

John 5:6–9

Then Peter said, "Silver or gold I do not have, but what I have I give you.
In the name of Jesus Christ of Nazareth, walk. . . . By faith in the name of
Jesus, this man whom you see and know was made strong. It is Jesus' name
and the faith that comes through him that has given this complete healing to
him, as you can all see."

Acts 3:6, 16

"Aeneas," Peter said to him, "Jesus Christ heals you. Get up and take
care of your mat." Immediately Aeneas got up.

Acts 9:34

Powerlessness in prayer is the mark of spiritual disease.

In the Christian life, just as in the physical life, powerlessness to walk is a symptom of some severe lack in the body that needs a doctor's attention. This lack of power to walk joyfully in the new and living way that leads to the Father and the throne of grace is especially devastating. Christ is the great Physician, who comes to every Bethesda where the sick are gathered and speaks out His loving, searching question: "Do you want to get well?"

For all who are still clinging to their hope in the pool or are looking for someone to put them in, for those who are hoping to be helped somehow in the course of time by the continued use of ordinary means of grace, His question points to a better way. He offers them healing by a way they have never understood. To all who are willing to confess not only their own powerlessness but also their failure to find anyone to help them, His question brings the sure and certain hope of deliverance.

We have seen that our weakness in prayer is part of a life afflicted with spiritual fruitlessness. Listen to our Lord as He offers to restore our spiritual strength, to fit us for walking like healthy, strong servants in all the ways of the Lord, and in that way to be well equipped to take our place in the great work of intercession. As we see what the wholeness is that He offers, how He gives it, and what He asks of us, we will be prepared to give a willing answer to His question.

The Health That Jesus Offers

There are many marks of spiritual health. Our text leads us to one: *walking*. Jesus said to the sick man, "Get up! . . . and walk." He restored the man to his place among men in full health and vigor, able to take his part in all the work of life. It is a wonderful picture of the restoration of spiritual health. To the healthy, walking is a pleasure; to the sick, it is a burden, if not an impossibility. To many Christians movement and progress in God's way is also a great effort and a burden. Christ comes to tell us, and with a word gives the power: "Get up! . . . and walk."

This walk to which He restores and empowers us is a life like that of Enoch and Noah, who "walked with God." And a life like Abraham's, to whom God said, "Walk before me," and who himself said, "The Lord before whom I walk." It is a life of which David sings, "They walk . . . in the light of your countenance," and Isaiah prophesies, "They that wait upon the Lord shall renew their strength . . . they shall run, and not be weary; and they shall walk, and not faint" (Isaiah 40:31 KJV).

God the Creator does not faint and is not weary, and they who walk with Him and wait on Him will never be exhausted or weak. It is a life reflective of the Old Testament saints Zechariah and Elisabeth, of whom it was said, "They were both righteous before God, walking in all the commandments and ordinances of the Lord blameless" (Luke 1:6 KJV). This is the walk Jesus came to make possible to His people in greater power than ever before.

The New Testament describes it: "As Christ was raised up from the dead by the glory of the Father, even so we also should walk in newness of life" (Romans 1:6 KJV). It is the Risen One who says to us, "Get up! . . . and walk." He gives us the power of the resurrection life. It is a walk *in* Christ: "As you have therefore received Christ Jesus the Lord, so walk in Him" (Colossians 2:6 NKJV). It is a walk *like* Christ: "He who says he abides in Him ought to walk just as He walked" (1 John 2:6 NKJV). It is a walk *in* the Spirit and *after* the Spirit: "Walk in the Spirit, and you shall not fulfill the lusts of the flesh . . . walk not after the flesh, but after the Spirit" (Galatians 5:16; Romans 8:1 NKJV). It is a walk worthy of God and well-pleasing to Him: "That you might walk worthy of the Lord unto all pleasing, being fruitful in every good work" (Colossians 1:10 KJV). It is a walk in love: "Walk in love, as Christ also hath loved us" (Ephesians 5:2 KJV). It is a walk of faith, its power coming from God the Father, the Son, and the Holy Spirit: "We walk by faith not by sight" (2 Corinthians 5:7 KJV).

How many believers regard such a walk as an impossible goal? So impossible that they do not feel it a sin to walk otherwise. Therefore, they do not truly desire this walk in newness of life. They have become so accustomed to the life of fruitlessness that the life and walk in God's strength has little attraction. There is no expectation of attaining it.

But there are some for whom this is not true. They wonder if these words mean what they say, if the life spoken of in these Scriptures is an unattainable ideal or if it is meant to be realized in this present life. The more they study the Scriptures, the more they are convinced that these admonitions are given for daily life. They appear idealistic, but how wonderful if this walk were truly possible.

God indeed sent His almighty Son and His Holy Spirit to call us and to prepare us for an earthly life to be lived with heavenly power beyond anything we could dare to imagine or hope for.

How Jesus Makes Us Whole

When a physician heals a patient, he acts from without, intending to render the patient independent of his doctor's aid.

The physician restores the patient to health and then leaves him. The work of our Lord Jesus is in both of these ways the very opposite. Jesus works not from without but from *within*. He enters by the power of His Spirit into our life.

Christ's purpose in healing is also the exact opposite of physical healing, which aims, if at all possible, toward independence from the doctors. Christ's condition of success is to bring us into such dependence upon himself that we will not be able to live a moment without Him.

Christ Jesus himself is our life in a sense that many Christians cannot conceive. The weak and frail Christian life owes itself to a lack of appropriation of divine truth. As long as we expect Christ to continually do something for us in single acts of grace, trusting Him from time to time to give us only that which will last a little while, we cannot be restored to perfect health. But when we grasp the fact that we need Him moment by moment in our lives in utter dependence upon His strength and provision, then the life of Christ becomes the health of our soul.

Health is nothing but life in its normal, undisturbed activity. Christ gives us health by giving us himself; He becomes our strength for our walk. Isaiah's words find their New Testament fulfillment: *They that wait on the Lord will walk and not faint, because Christ is the strength of their life.*

It is strange how believers sometimes think this life of dependence is too great a strain; they deplore a loss of personal liberty. They admit a need of dependence, but with room left over for the exercise of their own will and energy. They do not see that even a partial dependence makes them debtors and leaves them nothing to boast of. They forget that their relationship to God and cooperation with Him does not mean that He does the larger part and they the lesser, but that God does all and they do all—as one—God in me and I in God.

This dependence upon God secures one's true independence. When our will seeks nothing but the divine will, we reach a divine nobility, the true independence of all that is created. He that has not seen this will remain a sickly Christian—letting self do part and Christ do part. He that accepts the life of unceasing dependence on Christ as his life is made whole.

As God, Christ can enter and become the life of His creature. As the Glorified One, who received the Holy Spirit from the Father in order to give it away, Christ can renew the heart of sinful humanity. He can make it His home, and by His presence maintain it in full health and strength.

You who desire to walk in a way that pleases God, and not have your heart condemn you in your prayer life, listen to Christ's words: "Do you want to be made well?" He can give soul-health. He can give a life that prays, that is well-pleasing to the Father. If you want this life, hear how you can receive it.

What Christ Asks of Us

The opening text invites us to notice three specific things. Christ's question first appeals to the will and asks for its *consent*. Then He listens to our *confession* of utter helplessness. Next comes the *response* to Christ's command: the immediate obedience that gets up and walks.

First is the question "Do you want to get well?" Who wouldn't be willing to have his sickness taken away? But it is sad to see that there is a need to repeat the question. Some will not admit that they are sick. Some can believe others are sick—but not they! And some will not believe that Christ can make a person whole. *You must tell Him you want to be made well.*

At the root of it all is the fear of self-denial and the sacrifice that will be required. People are not willing to entirely give up their walk after the course of this world: to give up self-will, self-confidence, and self-pleasing. The walk in Christ that makes us like Christ is too straight and too hard. They do not want to be made whole. If you are willing to be made whole, you must confess clearly, "Lord, at any price, I will!" From Christ's side, the act is also one of the will: "I will; be clean." From your side equally: "May it be as you will."

Then the second step: Christ wants you to *look to Him as your only help*: "I have no one to put me in the water" must be your cry. Here on earth there is no help for you. Weakness may change into strength with normal care if all the organs and functions of the body are in a sound state. But sickness needs special measures. In the spiritual realm, your soul is sick; your inability to maintain a joyful Christian walk in God's way is a sign of disease. Do not be afraid to confess it and admit that there is no hope for you unless Christ in His mercy heals you. Give up the idea of simply changing from your sickly state into a healthy one, of growing out from under the law into a life under grace.

A few days ago I heard a student defend the cause of a missionary outreach. "The mission calls you," he said, "to a decision. Do not think that you will simply grow into a missionary. Unless God forbids you, take the step. The decision itself will bring joy and strength. It will set you free to prepare to go and to serve in the capacity of a missionary. And there is no calculating the help it will be to others." It is like that in the Christian life. You must choose. You must decide. Delay and struggle will only hinder you.

Confess that you cannot bring yourself to pray as you would like, because you do not give yourself to the healthy spiritual life that loves to pray and that knows how to count upon God's Spirit to pray through you. Come to Christ to heal you. In one moment He can make you whole, not in the sense of a sudden change in your feelings, but He will take charge of your inner life and fill it with himself and His Spirit.

The third thing Christ asks of us is the *response of faith.* When He spoke to the invalid, His command had to be obeyed. The man believed that there was truth and power in Christ's word; in that faith he got up and walked. By faith he obeyed. What Christ said to others was for him too—"Go your way; your faith has made you whole." Christ asks this faith of us. His Word changes our weakness into strength and equips us for that walk in newness of life for which we have been empowered by Him.

If we do not believe this, if we cannot with Paul have the courage to say, "I can do all things through Christ which strengthens me," we cannot fully obey. But if we will listen to the word that tells us of the walk that is not only possible but has been proven by the saints of old, if we will fix our gaze on Christ, who speaks with authority, "Get up and walk," we will have the courage to obey. We will stand and we will walk in Him and in His strength. We will know and tell and prove that Jesus Christ has made us whole.

Beware of forming wrong expectations of what must take place. When the man at the pool was made whole, he still had to learn everything about how to use his new strength. If he wanted to learn a trade, he had to start at the beginning. Do not expect to be all at once proficient in prayer or any part of the Christian life. Only be confident that as you have trusted yourself to Christ to be your spiritual health and strength, He will guide you and teach you.

Begin to pray. You must start. Count on the fact that He will work in you what you need. Rise and walk each day in the confidence that He is with you.

Chapter 9

The Secret of Effective Prayer

"Therefore I tell you, whatever you ask for in prayer, believe that you have received it, and it will be yours."

Mark 11:24

This text is a summary of our Lord Jesus' teaching on prayer. Nothing will so greatly help to convince us of the sin of our lack of prayer, to reveal its cause, and to give us courage to expect entire deliverance, as the careful study and acceptance of this teaching.

The more heartily we enter into the mind of our blessed Lord and set ourselves to think about prayer as He did, the more surely will His words be as living seeds. They will grow and produce in us their fruit—a life and practice that corresponds to the divine truth they contain. Let us believe this: Christ, the living Word of God, gives in His words a divine quickening power that brings into being what they say. It works in us what He asks, and actually fits and enables us for all He demands. Learn to view His teaching on prayer as a promise of what He, by His Holy Spirit, is going to work into your very being.

Our Lord gives us five essential elements of true prayer: (1) There must be the heart's *desire*; (2) there must be the expression of that desire in *prayer*; (3) there must be *faith* to carry the prayer to God; (4) there must be faith to *accept God's answer*; (5) *the experience* of the desired blessing must follow.

It may help to clarify our thinking if we take a specific request about which to learn to pray in faith. Better yet, we should unite together in the one thing that has been currently occupying our attention. For instance, after speaking about failure in prayer, or lack of prayer, why not take that as the object of our desire and intercession? We could say, "I want to ask and receive by faith the power to pray in the way God expects of me and as often as He expects." Let us meditate on our Lord's words:

1. "Whatever *you ask* . . ." We ask what we desire. Desire is the power that moves the whole world and directs the course of humankind. Desire is the soul of prayer, and the cause of insufficient or unsuccessful prayer is often because of a lack of desire. Some may doubt this, saying they have earnestly desired what they asked. But if they truly think about whether their desire has been as wholehearted as God would have it, they may discover that a lack of desire was indeed the cause of their failure.

"You will seek me and find me when you seek me with all your heart" (Jeremiah 29:13). It is written of Judah in the days of Asa, "They sought God eagerly, and he was found by them" (2 Chronicles 15:15).

A Christian may have a very strong desire for spiritual blessing, but a large part of his interests and affections are taken up with daily life. In other words, his spiritual desires are not all-consuming. He is puzzled that his prayer is not heard, but it is because God wants your whole heart. "The Lord our God is one Lord; and you shall love the Lord your God with all your heart." The law is unchangeable; God offers himself, gives himself, to the wholehearted who wholly give themselves to Him. He always gives us according to our heart's desire—not as we think of our desire, but as He sees it. If there are other desires that are more deeply a part of us, which occupy our heart more than He does, He will grant those desires, and the ones we ask halfheartedly in prayer cannot be granted.

If we desire the gift of intercession, grace, and power to pray aright, our hearts must be drawn away from lesser things; we must give ourselves wholly to what is most important. We must be willing to live to intercede for the kingdom. By focusing on the need of this grace, by believing with certainty that God will give it to us, by surrendering our very lives for the sake of a perishing world, our desire may be strengthened. The first step will have been taken toward the possession of the coveted blessing. Let us seek the grace of prayer as we seek with our whole heart the God with whom it will link us. We may depend upon the promise "He fulfills the desire of all who fear Him." Let us not fear to say, "I desire it with my whole heart."

2. "Whatever you ask for *in prayer* . . ." The desire of the heart must become the expression of the mouth. Our Lord Jesus more than once asked those who cried to Him for mercy, "What do you want?" He wanted them to tell him what they wanted. To declare it stirred their whole being into action, brought them into contact with Him, and awakened their expectation. To pray is to

enter into God's presence, to claim and secure His attention, to commit our need to His faithfulness, and to leave it there. It is in so doing that we become fully conscious of what we are asking.

There are some who have strong desires in their heart without bringing them to God in a clear expression of specific prayer. There are others who go to the Word and its promises to strengthen their faith but who do not actually ask God what they desire Him to do. Still others come in prayer with so many requests and desires that it is difficult even for them to say what they really expect of God.

If you want God to give you the gift of faithfulness in prayer and power to pray aright, begin to pray about that. Declare to God and to yourself, "Here is something I have asked and am continuing to ask until I receive it. As plain and pointed as words can make it, I am saying, 'My Father! I do desire, I do ask of you, and expect of you, the grace of prayer and intercession.'"

3. "Whatever you ask for in prayer, *believe . . .*" It is only by faith that we can know God or receive Jesus Christ or live the Christian life. So also faith is the life and power of prayer. If we are to begin a life of intercession in which there is to be joy and power and blessing, if we are to have our prayer for the grace of prayer answered, we must learn afresh what faith is and begin to live and pray in faith as never before.

Faith is the opposite of sight, and the two are contrary to each other. "We walk by faith and not by sight" (2 Corinthians 5:7 KJV). If the unseen is to gain full possession of us, and our hearts and lives and prayers are to be full of faith, there must be a withdrawal from the visible. The one who seeks to enjoy as much as possible of what is supposedly innocent or legitimate, who gives first place to the cares and duties of daily life, is inconsistent with a strong faith and close relationship to the spiritual world. "We *look not* at the things that are seen"—the negative action needs to be emphasized if the positive, "but at the things that are not seen," is to become natural to us. In praying, faith depends upon our living in the invisible world.

This faith refers especially to faith in God. The biggest reason for our lack of faith is our lack of knowledge of God and communion with Him. "Have faith in God," Jesus said when He spoke of removing mountains. When a soul knows God, is occupied with His power, love, and faithfulness, comes out of self and the world and allows the light of God to illuminate his mind, unbelief will become impossible. All the mysteries and difficulties connected with answers to prayer—however little we may be able to solve them intellectually—will be swallowed up in the assurance, "This God is our God. He will bless us. He does indeed answer prayer. And the grace to pray that I am asking for He will delight to give."

4. "Whatever you ask for in prayer, believe that *you have received it*." Faith has to accept the answer as given by God in heaven before it is found or felt on earth. This point causes difficulty but it is the essence of believing prayer. Try to understand: Spiritual things can only be grasped or appropriated by the spirit. God's answer to your prayer must be recognized and accepted in your spirit before you know it in reality. It is faith that accomplishes this.

A person who not only seeks an answer but seeks first the God who gives the answer will know that he has obtained what he asked. If he knows that he has asked according to God's will, he can believe that he has received.

There is nothing so heart-searching as the path to acknowledging *I believe that I have received it.* As we strive to believe and find that we cannot, it leads us to discover what it is that hinders our believing. Blessed is the man who holds nothing back, who with his eye and heart on God alone, refuses to rest until he has believed what the Word says: "Whatever you ask for in prayer, *believe* that you have received it." It is here that Jacob becomes Israel, and the power of prevailing prayer is born out of human weakness and despair. Persevering, persistent prayer will not rest or give up until it knows it is heard and believes that it has received.

Are you praying for the Spirit of grace and supplication? Believe that all the pressures of daily life that tend to hinder prayer can be overcome. Believe that God will give you your heart's desire: grace to pray in the Spirit as much and as long as the Father would have you do.

5. "Whatever you ask for in prayer, believe that you have received it, and *it will be yours.*" Receiving something from God by faith—believing in the answer with perfect assurance that it has already been given—is not necessarily the experience itself or the actual possession of what we have asked for. At times there may be a considerable wait involved. In other cases the believer may enjoy immediately what he has asked. Of course, in the case of having to wait for the answer, we have a greater need for faith and patience. We need faith to rejoice and be thankful for the answer, even though we have nothing tangible to show we have been heard.

We need this faith to be effective intercessors, for grace to pray earnestly and persistently for the lost or needy around us. We must hold fast the divine assurance that as surely as we believe, we will receive. The more we praise God for the answer, the sooner it will be ours. Begin now to pray for others in the confidence that grace will be given to pray with more perseverance and more faith than ever before.

If you do not immediately see an increase in your desire to pray, do not allow circumstances to hinder or discourage you. Even without any change in feelings, you have accepted the spiritual gift by faith. The Holy Spirit may seem hidden, but you may count on Him to pray through you, even if it is only sighing. In due time you will become conscious again of His full presence and power.

Ask God. Believe that you have received what you ask. If you still find it difficult to do this, say that you believe on the strength of His Word.

"Believe that you have received." Begin with the faith you have, even though weak. Step by step, be faithful in prayer and intercession. The more simply you hold to this truth and expect the Holy Spirit to work, the more surely will the Word be made true for you.

Chapter 10

The Spirit of Supplication

"I will pour out on the house of David and the inhabitants of Jerusalem a spirit of grace and supplication."

Zechariah 12:10

In the same way, the Spirit helps us in our weakness. We do not know what we ought to pray for, but the Spirit himself intercedes for us with groans that words cannot express. And he who searches our hearts knows the mind of the Spirit, because the Spirit intercedes for the saints in accordance with God's will.

Romans 8:26–27

And pray in the Spirit on all occasions with all kinds of prayers and requests. With this in mind, be alert and always keep on praying for all the saints.

Ephesians 6:18

Pray in the Holy Spirit.

Jude 20

The Holy Spirit has been given to every child of God. He dwells in him not as a separate being in one part of his nature but as his very life. He is the divine power or energy by which our life is maintained and strengthened. The Holy Spirit can and will work in a believer all that one is called to be or to do. Of course, the person on his part must yield to the Holy Spirit. Without this, He cannot work, and the person's spiritual life will be less than effective. But as he learns to yield, to wait, and to obey the leading of the Spirit, God will work in him all that is pleasing in His sight.

The Holy Spirit, above all, is a Spirit of prayer. He is given as the "Spirit of grace and supplication." When He is present, our heart cries, "Abba, Father." And in true faith and growing understanding He enables us to say, "Our Father, who art in heaven."

"He makes intercession for the saints according to the will of God." As we pray in the Spirit, our worship is as God desires it to be, "in spirit and in truth." Prayer is simply the breathing of the Spirit in us; power in prayer comes from the power of the Spirit in us as we wait on Him. Failure in prayer is the result of a spirit that is not yielded to the Spirit of God. In this sense, prayer is a gauge that measures the work of the Spirit in us. To pray aright, the life of the Spirit must be active in us. For praying the effective, fervent prayer of a righteous man, everything depends on being full of the Spirit.

The believer who would enjoy the blessing of being taught to pray by the Spirit of prayer must know four very simple things:

First, *believe that the Spirit dwells in you* (Ephesians 1:13). Deep in the inmost recesses of his being, hidden and unfelt, every child of God has the mighty Spirit of God. He knows it by faith, by accepting God's Word on the matter, even when he sees no sign of it.

We receive the promise of the Spirit through faith. As long as we measure our power to pray persistently and in the right way by what we feel or think we can accomplish, we will be discouraged. But when we believe that the Holy Spirit—the Spirit of supplication—is dwelling within us in the midst of all our conscious weakness *for the very purpose of enabling us to pray,* our hearts will be filled with hope. We will be strengthened with the assurance that lies at the root of a happy and fruitful Christian life: *God has made abundant provision for our being what He wants us to be.* We will begin to lose our burden, our fear, our discouragement about our ever praying sufficiently, because we will see that the Holy Spirit prays in us.

Second, *beware, above everything, of grieving the Holy Spirit* (Ephesians 4:30). If you grieve Him, how can He work in you the quiet, blessed sense of union with Christ that makes your prayers well pleasing to the Father? Beware of grieving Him through sin, unbelief, selfishness, or unfaithfulness to His voice through your conscience.

But never think grieving Him is inevitable. That idea cuts through the very sinews of your strength to obey the command. Do not consider it impossible to obey the words "Do not grieve the Holy Spirit." He is the power of God to make you obedient. Sins that crop up against your will: a tendency to laziness, pride, self-will, or inordinate affection, can be at once rejected in the power of the Spirit and cast upon Christ and His blood. Then communion with God is restored.

Each day accept the Holy Spirit as your guide, your life, and your strength, the one who reveals Christ to you. He, unseen but known by faith, gives all the love, faith, and power for obedience that you need. Do not grieve Him by distrusting Him, even when you cannot feel His presence in you.

The best and truest prayer is to put yourself before God just as you are and to count on the Spirit who prays within you. Prayer that is easy and powerful and joyful may not come all at once. Humble yourself before God.

"We do not know what we ought to pray for." This is common to us all. Our human weakness includes ignorance, difficulties, and struggles of many kinds. "But the Spirit helps us in our weakness." How is this possible? "The Spirit himself intercedes for us with groans that words cannot express. And he who searches our hearts knows the mind of the Spirit, because the Spirit intercedes for the saints in accordance with God's will." When you cannot find the words, or when your words seem cold and meaningless, believe that the Holy Spirit is praying in you.

Be quiet before God. Give Him time and opportunity to speak to you. In due season you will learn to pray. Honor Him in patient, trustful surrender to His intercession in you.

Third, *be filled with the Spirit* (Ephesians 5:18). I think we have by now learned a great truth: It is only the healthy spiritual life that can pray as it should. Though some may be content with only a small measure of the Spirit's working, it is God's will that we should be filled with the Spirit. From our perspective, that means our whole being ought to be entirely yielded to the Holy Spirit to be guided and controlled by Him alone. From God's side, we can count on and expect the Holy Spirit to take full possession of our being and fill us with power and love for intercession.

If prayer is not answered, perhaps it is due to our not having accepted the Spirit of prayer to be our voice; to our having failed to yield wholly to Him. The Father gave us the Spirit of His Son so that He might work the life of the Son in us. Let us gladly receive Him, yielding ourselves to Him and trusting Him to fill us with himself. Let us not willfully grieve the Holy Spirit by declining, neglecting, or hesitating to have Him as fully as He is willing to give himself to us. If we have seen that prayer is the greatest need of our work and of the church, or if we have desired or resolved to pray more, let us turn to the source of all power and blessing. Let us believe that the Spirit of prayer in His fullness is for us.

We all agree as to the place the Father and the Son have in our prayers. It is to the Father we pray, and from whom we expect the answer. It is in the merit, the name, and life of the Son, by our abiding in Him and He in us, that we trust to be heard. But have we understood that in the Holy Trinity all three persons have an equal place in prayer? Faith in the Holy Spirit of intercession as He prays in us is as indispensable as our faith in the Father and the Son. How clearly we see this in the words "Through [Christ] we both have access by one Spirit unto the Father." As much as prayer must be *to* the Father and *through* the Son, it must be *by* the Spirit. The Spirit can pray through us only as He is allowed to live in us.

Our third and final requirement for prayer is to *pray in the Spirit for all the saints* (Ephesians 6:18). The Spirit, who is called the Spirit of supplication, is also the Spirit of intercession. Remember, it is said of Him, "The Spirit himself intercedes for us with groans that words cannot express" and "the Spirit intercedes for the saints in accordance with God's will."

The thought in these verses is essentially that of mediation— one person pleading for another. When the Spirit of intercession takes full possession of us, all selfishness—wanting Him apart from His intercession—is banished, and we begin to avail ourselves of our wonderful privilege to plead for all the saints. We long to live the Christ-life of self-consuming sacrifice for others. Our heart unceasingly yields itself to God to obtain His blessing for those around us. Intercession then becomes not an incidental or an occasional part of our prayers but their one great object. Prayer for ourselves takes its place as a means of preparing us to be more effective in the exercise of our ministry of intercession.

I have humbly asked God to give me what I need in order to give you divine enlightenment and help to forsake the life of ordinary prayer—words without faith or direction—and enter into the life of intercession that the Holy Spirit desires you to have. By a simple act of faith, claim the fullness of the Spirit you are capable in God's sight of receiving and which He is therefore willing to bestow. Will you not, even now, receive it by faith?

What takes place at conversion? Most of you for a time sought peace by struggling to give up sin and please God. But you did not find it that way. The peace of God's pardon came by faith, by trusting God's Word concerning Christ and His salvation. You had heard of Christ as the gift of God's love, and you felt the drawing of His grace. But not until by faith in God's Word you accepted Christ as your own did you know the peace and joy that He can give. Believing in Him and His saving love has made all the difference and changed your relationship from one who grieved Him to one who loves and serves Him. Yet you have many times thought that you love and serve Him far less than He deserves.

At the time of your conversion you may have known little

about the Holy Spirit. Later you learned that He actually dwells in you and is the power of God to make you all that the Father intends you to be. In spite of all this, His indwelling and inworking may seem vague and indefinite, and rarely a source of joy or strength. At conversion you did not yet know of your need of Him and still less what to expect of Him. But your failures have taught you. Now you are beginning to see how you have grieved Him by not allowing Him to work in you all of God's good pleasure.

All of this can be changed. After seeking Christ, praying to Him, and trying without success to serve Him as you know you should, you found rest in accepting Him by faith. Even now you may yield yourself to the full guidance of the Holy Spirit and accept His working in you what God would have. Will you do it? Accept Him as Christ's gift to you, His Spirit in you to be your life, including your prayer life. You can count on Him to take charge. No matter how weak or unable to pray effectively you feel, you can bow before God with full assurance that He will teach you to pray.

Just as you by conscious faith accepted Christ's pardon, you can now consciously receive by faith the Holy Spirit. Christ has redeemed us that we might receive the promise of the Spirit by faith. Acknowledge the Spirit's presence in you by reason of your conversion and simply believe that the Lord Christ, who baptizes with the Holy Spirit, now, in response to your faith, will begin in you a full experience of the power of the indwelling Spirit. Depend upon Him, apart from any feeling or past experience, as the spirit of supplication and intercession. Renew that act of faith each morning, each time you pray. Trust Him, against all appearances, to work in you—be assured He is working—and He will reveal to you the joy of the Holy Spirit as the power of your life.

The mystery of prayer is the mystery of the divine indwelling. God the Father gives His Spirit in our hearts to be the divine power that prays in us and draws us toward Him. God is Spirit, and nothing but the Spirit within us can allow us to have communion with Him.

It was for communion with God that man was created. God dwelling in us gives us His life. It was this divine indwelling that was lost through sin. Christ died to win it back for us. It is this indwelling of God through His Spirit that alone can enable us to appropriate the wonderful promises given with regard to prayer. God gives us the Spirit of supplication to maintain His divine life within us out of which prayer continually rises.

Without the Holy Spirit, none of us can call Jesus Lord or cry, "Abba, Father," and no one can worship in spirit and truth or pray without ceasing. The Holy Spirit is given to the believer to be and do in him all that God desires. He is given especially as the Spirit of prayer and supplication. It is clear that everything in prayer depends upon our trusting the Holy Spirit to do His work in us.

We read that Stephen was "a man full of faith and the Holy Spirit" (Acts 6:5 NKJV). The two always go together, in exact proportion to each other. As our faith sees and trusts the Spirit in us to pray, and waits on Him, He will do what we cannot do on our own. It is genuine desire, fervent supplication, and childlike faith the Father seeks. Let us learn to know the Spirit, and in the faith of Christ, who continuously gives Him, cultivate the confidence that we can learn to pray as the Father would have us pray.

Chapter 11

In the Name of Christ

"And I will do whatever you ask in my name, so that the Son may bring glory to the Father. The Father will give you whatever you ask in my name. I tell you the truth, my Father will give you whatever you ask in my name. Until now you have not asked for anything in my name. Ask and you will receive, and your joy will be complete. In that day you will ask in my name."

John 14:13; 15:16; 16:23–24, 26

"In my name" is repeated five times in our text. Our Lord knew how slow our hearts would be to take it in, but He so longed that we would believe that His name is the power under which every knee should bow, and by which every prayer could be heard. He did not become weary of saying over and over, "in my name"! Between the wonderful "whatever you ask" and the divine "I will do it" is the simple link "in my name." Our asking and the Father's giving are both in the name of Christ. Everything in prayer depends upon our grasping what it means to pray "in His name."

A name calls to mind the whole being and nature of a person

or thing. When I speak of a lamb or a lion, the name at once suggests the nature peculiar to each. The name of God is meant to express His divine nature and glory. So also the name of Christ means His nature, His person and work, His disposition and Spirit. To ask in the name of Christ is to pray in union with Him.

When a sinner first believes in Christ, he thinks only of His merit—and to the very end that is the one foundation of our confidence. But as the believer grows in grace and enters more deeply into union with Christ—as he abides in Him—he learns that to pray in the name of Christ also means to pray in His Spirit.

As we grasp the meaning of the words "In that day you will ask in my name"—speaking of the day when, by the Spirit, Christ came to live in His disciples—we will no longer be staggered at the greatness of the promise: "*Whatever* you ask in my name, that will I do." We will gain some insight into the unchangeable certainty of the law: *Whatever is asked in the name of Christ—in union with Him, out of His nature and Spirit—must be given.*

As Christ's prayer nature lives in us, His prayer power becomes ours as well. The measure of our attainment or experience is not the ground of our confidence; it is the wholeheartedness of our surrender to all that Christ seeks to be in us. If we abide in Him, He says, we can ask whatever we desire.

As we live in Him, we receive the spiritual power to avail ourselves of His name. As the branch wholly surrendered to the life and service of the vine can count upon its sap and strength for its fruit, so the believer who in faith has accepted the fullness of the Spirit to possess his whole life, benefits from the power of Christ's name.

Christ came to earth as a man to reveal what true prayer is. To pray in the name of Christ, we must pray as He prayed. He taught us to pray in union with Him. Let us in love and faith accept Him as our example, our teacher, and our intercessor.

Christ Our Example

Christ's prayer on earth and His prayer in us cannot be two different prayers, in the sense that there is but one spirit of acceptable prayer. Christ spent a great deal of time in prayer while on earth; all the great events of His life were connected together by prayer. If we would live a spiritual life and exercise spiritual power, we must learn the necessity of absolute dependence upon and unceasing communication with the spiritual world through Christ.

It is easy to see how foolish and fruitless is the attempt to do work for God without first going to Him in prayer to get His mind and will in the matter. Unless this truth lives in us, we cannot avail ourselves of the mighty power of the name of Christ. His example teaches us the meaning of His name.

When He was baptized, Jesus prayed, and heaven was opened. It was through prayer that heaven came down to Him by the Spirit and in the voice of His Father. In the power of the Spirit He was led into the wilderness, to fasting and prayer, to be tested and to be fully prepared for his ministry.

Early in His ministry, Mark records (1:35), "Very early in the morning, while it was still dark, Jesus got up, left the house and went off to a solitary place, where he prayed." Somewhat later Luke tells us (5:15–16) "crowds of people came to hear him and to be healed of their sicknesses. But Jesus often withdrew to lonely places and prayed."

As a man, Jesus knew how even the service of preaching and healing can exhaust the spirit, how constant contact with humanity can cloud our fellowship with God. He knew that much time was needed if the Spirit was to abide in Him. He recognized that no pressure of responsibility to people could excuse Him from the absolute need of extended prayer.

If anyone could have been satisfied with always living and working in the Spirit of prayer, it would have been our Master. But He did not take it for granted; He needed to have His spiritual supply replenished by continual and lengthy seasons of prayer. To use Christ's name in prayer includes following His example and to pray as He did.

Concerning the night before choosing His apostles, we read (Luke 6:12): "One of those days Jesus went out to a mountainside to pray, and spent the night praying to God." The first step toward the establishment of the church and the separation of certain ones to be His witnesses and successors required special prolonged prayer. All had to be done according to the pattern Jesus revealed: "The Son can do nothing of himself . . . but what he sees the Father do." It was in the night of prayer that the instructions were given Him.

In the night between feeding the five thousand—when Jesus knew the people wanted to take Him by force and make Him king—and walking on the sea: "After he had dismissed them, he went up on a mountainside by himself to pray. When evening came, he was there alone" (Matthew 14:23). He had come to do God's will and to reveal God's power. He did not possess it in himself; it had to be prayed for and received from above.

The first announcement of Christ's approaching death, after He had drawn from Peter the confession that He was the Christ, is introduced by the words (Luke 9:18) "When Jesus was praying in private. . . ." The introduction to the story of the Transfiguration says (Luke 9:28), "He . . . went up onto a mountain to pray." The request of the disciples, "Lord, teach us to pray" (Luke 11:1), follows the statement, "One day Jesus was praying in a certain place." In His own personal life, in His relationship with the Father, in all He is and does for us, the Christ whose name we are to use was and is a man of prayer.

It is prayer that gives Christ His power to bless and transfigures His body with the glory of heaven. It is His prayer life that qualifies Him to teach others how to pray. How much more must prayer alone before the Father fit us to share His glory of a transfigured life and make us a channel of blessing and teaching to others. To pray in the name of Christ is to pray as He prays.

As Christ's death approached, He prayed even more. When the Greeks asked to see Him, and He spoke of His approaching death, He prayed again. At Lazarus's grave He prayed. In His last night on earth He prayed His prayer as our High Priest that we might know what His sacrifice would win and what His everlasting intercession on the throne would be. In Gethsemane He prayed His prayer as the victim—the Lamb giving itself to the slaughter. On the cross it was still prayer: the prayer of compassion for His murderers, the prayer of atoning suffering in the darkness, the prayer in death of the resignation of His spirit to the Father's will.

Christ's life and work, His suffering and death, were founded on prayer—total dependence upon God the Father, trust in God, receiving from God, and surrendering to God. Your redemption is brought into being by prayer and intercession. The life He lived *for* you and the life He lives *in* you is a life that delights to wait on God and receive from Him. To pray in His name is to pray as He prayed. Christ is our example because He is our Head, our Savior, and our Life. In virtue of His deity and of His Spirit, He can live in us. We can pray in His name because we abide in Him and He abides in us.

Christ Our Teacher

Christ was everything He taught. His teaching was simply the revelation of how He lived and of the life He was to live in us. His teaching the disciples was intended to awaken desire for God in them and so prepare them for what He would by the Holy Spirit work through them. Let us be confident that all He was in prayer and all He taught others, He himself will give to us. He came to fulfill the law; how much more will He fulfill the Gospel in all that He teaches us in prayer.

1. *What to pray.* It has sometimes been said that direct petitions, as compared with the exercise of fellowship with God, are but a subordinate part of prayer, and that in the prayer of those who pray best, they occupy a very small space. If we carefully study all that our Lord spoke of prayer, however, we will see that this was not His teaching. In the Lord's Prayer, the parables on prayer, the illustration of a child asking for bread, of our seeking and knocking, and in the central thought of the prayer of faith: "Whatever you ask in prayer believing you will receive"—even in

the oft-repeated *whatever* of the last evening—our Lord urges and encourages us to offer definite petitions and to expect definite answers.

Only because we have so often confined prayer to our own needs has it been thought necessary to free prayer from the appearance of selfishness by giving petitions a subordinate place. Believers need to wake up to the glory of the work of intercession. We need to see that in it and in the definite pleading for particular gifts on particular spheres and persons lay our highest fellowship with our glorified Lord and our only real power to bless others. It will then become clear that there can be no truer fellowship with God than through our petitions and their answers by which we become the channel of His grace and life to others. By intercession our fellowship with the Father can be such as the Son has with the Father in His intercession.

2. *How to pray.* Our Lord taught us to pray in private, in simplicity, with our eye on God alone, in humility and in the spirit of forgiving love. But the primary truth He taught about prayer was this: *Pray in faith.* He defined faith not only as trust in God's goodness and power but as the assurance that we have received the very thing we ask of Him. Then in view of delays in the answer, he taught perseverance and urgency in prayer.

We must be followers of those "who through faith and patience inherit the promises" (Hebrews 6:12 NKJV). We must exercise the faith that accepts the promise and knows it has what it has asked, while at the same time when there is a delay, practice the patience that obtains the promise and inherits the blessing. We will then learn to understand why God, who promises to avenge His elect quickly, bears with them through seeming delay.

It is surely so that their faith may be purified from all that is of the flesh and tested and strengthened to become that spiritual power that can even cast mountains into the sea.

Christ Our Intercessor

We have seen in Scripture how Christ prayed while on earth and we have heard His teaching as to how we must pray. But to truly know what it means to pray in His name, we must know something of His heavenly intercession.

Consider the fact that all of Christ's saving work continues to be accomplished from heaven just as it was while He was on earth in unceasing communication with and direct intercession to the Father, who works it all out among all who seek Him. Every act of grace in Christ has been preceded by and owes its power to intercession. God is honored and acknowledged as its author.

On the throne of God, Christ's highest fellowship with the Father and His partnership in His rule of the world is in intercession. Every blessing that reaches us from above bears the stamp of Christ's intercession. His prayer for us is the fruit and glory of His atonement. When He gave himself as a sacrifice to God for us, He proved that His whole heart had one objective—the glory of God in the salvation of men. In His intercession this great purpose is realized: He glorifies the Father by asking and receiving from Him, and He saves men by bestowing what He obtains from the Father.

Christ our Intercessor is our life. He is our Head and we are His body. His Spirit and life breathe in us. As in heaven so on earth, intercession is God's chosen channel of blessing. Let us learn from Christ what glory there is in this kind of prayer.

1. *The glory of intercession.* Beyond anything else, we glorify God through intercession. By it we bring blessing to the church and to the world. By it we have our highest honor—the power to be God's instrument in saving souls.

2. *The way to intercession.* Paul wrote, "Walk in love, as Christ has loved us and given himself for us an offering and a sacrifice to God." If we live as Christ lived, we will give ourselves to God to be used by Him for the sake of others. Once we have done this, no more to seek anything for ourselves but for others, intercession will become for us, as it was and is for Christ, the great work of our life.

And when and if the call seems too high or the work too hard, the interceding Christ, who lives in us, will give us the victory. We will hear Him say, "The works that I do, you will do also, and greater works than these." Let us not forget that we are not under the law, which is powerless, but under grace. We can claim afresh the fullness of God's Spirit as His all-sufficient provision for our need. We can count on Him to be in us the Spirit of intercession.

When we understand the part intercession plays in God's work through us, we will no longer try to work for God and ask Him to bless it. We will do what the friend at midnight did, ask until we receive in order that others may have what God has to offer.

As Christ did, we must make it our primary effort to receive from the Father. No time or trouble will be too great to serve others by prayer and intercession.

Be of good courage as servants of Christ and children of God.

Let no weakness or any lack cause you to fear—simply ask in the name of Christ. His name has all the power of Christ himself. His promise still stands: "You may ask me for anything in my name, and I will do it."

Chapter 12

My God Will Hear Me

Yet the LORD longs to be gracious to you; he rises to show you compassion. For the LORD is a God of justice. Blessed are all who wait for him! O people of Zion, who live in Jerusalem, you will weep no more. How gracious he will be when you cry for help! As soon as he hears, he will answer you.

Isaiah 30:18–19

Know that the LORD has set apart the godly for himself; the LORD will hear when I call to him.

Psalm 4:3

I call on you, O God, for you will answer me; give ear to me and hear my prayer.

Psalm 17:6

But as for me, I watch in hope for the LORD, I wait for God my Savior; my God will hear me.

Micah 7:7

The power of prayer rests in the faith that God hears our prayers. This is true in more than one sense. It is this faith that gives us courage to pray; that gives us power to prevail with God. The moment I am assured that God hears *me*, I feel drawn to pray and to persevere in prayer. I feel strong to claim and to take by faith the answer God gives. One of the great reasons for lack of prayer is the lack of a living, joyous assurance that God hears us. If only we could get a vision of the living God waiting with open arms to grant our request. Wouldn't we then set aside everything to make time and space for the prayer of faith?

When a man can and does declare in living faith, "My God will hear me!" surely nothing will keep him from prayer. He knows that what he cannot do on earth can and will be done for him in heaven. Let us bow in quietness before God and wait on Him until He reveals himself as the God who hears. In His presence this central truth will become clear to us.

1. *"My God will hear me."* What a blessed certainty! We are assured of it by many promises in His Word. We also have innumerable witnesses to the fact. How many have not experienced it in their lives? The Son of God has given us the clear message that if we ask, the Father will give us what we desire. Christ sits at the right hand of the Father making intercession for us. God *delights* in hearing our prayers. He has allowed us many times to be tried that we might be compelled to cry to Him and to know Him as the God who hears prayer.

Let us confess with shame how we have often doubted this wondrous truth. And then let us come before Him as an earthly child does his parent and say, "I know my father hears me."

By experience you know how little an intellectual understanding of truth has profited you. Ask God to *reveal* himself to you. If you want to live a different prayer life, worship God in silence before you make your petition. Wait until a deep consciousness of His nearness and readiness to answer is felt.

2. *What a wondrous grace!* Think of God in His infinite majesty, His altogether incomprehensible glory, His unapproachable holiness, sitting on a throne of grace, waiting to be gracious, inviting and encouraging you to pray.

Now think of yourself in your nothingness and helplessness as a mere creature, in your wretchedness and unworthiness as a sinner, and praise the glory of that grace that allows you to come boldly before the throne.

Think of what can be accomplished in the place of intimacy with God. God has united you with Christ. In Him and in His name you have full confidence. From the throne He prays with you and for you. At the footstool of the throne you pray with Him and in Him. His worth and the Father's delight in hearing Him are the measure of your confidence, your full assurance of being heard.

There is more. When you know not what to pray as you ought, think of the Holy Spirit, the Spirit of God's own Son within your heart, crying, *"Abba, Father."* He is the Spirit of supplication. In all your insignificance and unworthiness, you are as acceptable as Christ himself. In all your ignorance and weakness, the Spirit makes intercession according to God's will within you. What wondrous grace! Through Christ I have access to the Father, by the Spirit. I do believe my God will hear me.

3. *What a deep mystery!* There are difficulties that at times arise and perplex the honest heart. There is the question as to God's sovereign will. How can our wishes, often so foolish, and our will, often so selfish, overrule or change that perfect will? Would it not be better to leave all at His disposal, who knows

what is best and loves to give us the very best? Or how can our prayer change what He has before ordained?

The question arises too as to the need of persevering prayer and the long waiting for an answer. If God is infinite love and delights to give more than we delight to receive, why is there a need for pleading and wrestling, for the urgency and long delay of which Scripture and experience speak?

Arising out of this there is still another question—that of the multitude of vain and unanswered prayers. How many have pleaded for loved ones and they die without Christ. How many cry for years for spiritual blessing and no answer seems to come. To think of all this tries our faith and makes us hesitate to say, "My God will hear me."

Prayer, in its power with God, and His faithfulness to His promise to hear it, is a deep spiritual mystery. Some answers could be given that would remove some of the difficulty from the questions asked. But what must in any case be said is this: As little as we can comprehend God himself we can comprehend one of the most blessed promises—that He hears prayer. It is a spiritual mystery—nothing less.

God hears because we pray in His Son's name, because the Holy Spirit prays in us. If we have believed and claimed Christ as our life and the fullness of the Spirit as our strength, let us not hesitate to believe in the power of our prayer. The Holy Spirit can enable us to believe and to rejoice in it, even when every question is not yet answered. He will do this as we surrender our questions to God's love, trust His faithfulness, and give ourselves humbly to obey His command to pray without ceasing.

Every art unfolds its secrets and its beauty only to the one who practices it. To the humble soul who prays in the obedience of faith, who practices prayer and intercession diligently because God asks it, the mystery will be revealed. Then the thought of the deep secrets of prayer, instead of being a burdensome problem, will be a source of rejoicing, adoration, and faith, in which the unceasing refrain is ever heard, "My God will hear me."

4. *What a solemn responsibility!* Often we complain of darkness, of weakness, of failure, as if there was no help for it. Yet God has promised in answer to our prayer to supply our every need and to give us His light and strength and peace. If only we could realize the responsibility of having such a God and such promises and see the sin and shame of not availing ourselves of them to the utmost. How confident we would then feel that the grace we have accepted and trusted to enable us to pray as we should will be given.

This access to a prayer-hearing God is especially intended to make us intercessors. Christ obtained His right of prevailing intercession by His giving himself as a sacrifice to God for us, and through it receives the blessings He dispenses. Even so, if we have truly given ourselves to God for others, we share Christ's right of intercession and are able to obtain the powers of the heavenly world for those for whom we pray.

The power of life and death is in our hands (1 John 5:16). In answer to prayer, the Spirit can be poured out, souls can be converted, and believers can be established. Through prayer, the kingdom of darkness can be conquered, souls brought out of prison into the liberty of Christ, and the glory of God revealed. Through prayer, the sword of the Spirit, which is the Word of God, can be wielded in power; in public preaching as well as in private speaking, the most rebellious can be made to bow at Jesus' feet.

What a responsibility on the church to give herself to the work of intercession! What a responsibility on every minister, missionary, and layworker, set apart for the saving of souls, to yield themselves wholly to act out and prove their faith: "My God will hear me!" What a call on every believer: instead of burying and losing this talent, to seek to use it in prayer and supplication for all saints and for all others. The deeper our entrance into the truth of this wonderful power God has given to us, the more wholehearted will be our surrender to the work of intercession.

5. *What a blessed prospect!* I see now that all my failures in the past have been due to my lack of faith in the area of believing that God hears me. Especially in the work of intercession; I did not fully believe that God heard me. But praise God! I am beginning to see it and believe it. All will be so different now.

Ordinary and insignificant though I am, filling a very small place in His kingdom, even I have access to this infinite God with the confidence that He hears me. One with Christ and led by the Holy Spirit, I dare to say, "I will boldly pray for others, for I know God hears me."

What a blessed prospect indeed—every earthly and spiritual anxiety exchanged for the peace of God, who cares for all and hears our prayer. What a blessed prospect in my work—to know that even when the answer is delayed and there is a call for patient, persevering prayer, the truth remains the same: Our God hears us.

What a blessed prospect for Christ's church if we give prayer its proper place, or better, *give the prayer-hearing God His proper place!* This is what those who begin to awaken to the urgent need of prayer ought to pray for primarily: that Christ be given the right place in our lives.

When God first poured out the Spirit on His praying people, He laid down a decree for all time: In the degree that you pray, so will you receive of the Spirit. Let each one who can say, "My God hears me," join in the fervent supplication that throughout the church this truth may be restored to its rightful place and the blessed prospect be realized: A praying church will be endued with the power of the Holy Spirit.

6. *What a need for divine teaching!* We need this both to enable us to hold the Word in living faith and to make full use of it in intercession. It has been said—and cannot be said too often—that the one thing needful for the church of our day is the power of the Holy Spirit. As true as this is from the divine side, just as true from the human side is the fact that the one thing needed among us is more believing, persevering prayer.

Speaking of a lack of the Spirit's power and the condition for receiving it, someone said, "The blockage is not on the vertical but on the horizontal." It is to be feared that it is on both. There is much to be confessed and removed if the Spirit is to work freely. Though it is true there must be unity and fellowship among believers, there also needs to be a continual upward look and a deep dependence and strong crying to God, an effectual prayer of faith that avails—all these things are sadly lacking.

We must all strive to learn the lesson that will make prevailing prayer possible—the lesson of a faith that can sing, "My God hears me." Simple and elementary as it is, it needs practice and patience, time and heavenly teaching to learn this lesson well.

Under the impression of a passing thought or a blessed experience, it may look as if we knew the lesson perfectly. But over and
over the need will recur of making this our first prayer: that God
who hears prayer would teach us to believe it and so to pray as
we should.

If we desire revelation, we can count upon Him. He delights
in hearing prayer and answering it. He gave His Son that He
might always pray for us and with us, and that His Holy Spirit
might pray in us. We can be sure there is not a prayer that He
will hear more certainly than this: *Reveal yourself as the prayer-
hearing God that our whole being may respond to it and believe it.*

Chapter 13

Paul, a Model of Prayer

*The Lord told him, "Go to the house of Judas on Straight Street
and ask for a man from Tarsus named Saul, for he is praying."*

Acts 9:11

*But for that very reason I was shown mercy so that in me, the
worst of sinners, Christ Jesus might display his unlimited patience
as an example for those who would believe on him
and receive eternal life.*

1 Timothy 1:16

God took His own Son and made Him our example and our
model. Sometimes it seems as if the power of Christ's example is
lost in the thought that He, in whom there is no sin, is not a man
as we are.

Our Lord took Paul, a man of like passions with ourselves,
and made him a model of what Christ could do for one who
called himself the chief of sinners. And Paul, the man who more
than any other has left his mark on the church, has ever after
been appealed to as a model.

In his mastery of divine truth and his teaching of it, in his devotion to his Lord and his self-consuming zeal in His service, in his deep experience of the power of the indwelling Christ and the fellowship of His cross, in the sincerity of his humility and the simplicity and boldness of his faith, in his missionary enthusiasm and endurance—in all this and more, "the grace of our Lord was exceedingly abundant" in him.

Christ gave Paul, and the church has accepted him, as a model of what Christ desires in His disciples. Six times Paul speaks of believers following him: 1 Corinthians 4:16: "Therefore I urge you to imitate me"; 1 Corinthians 11:1: "Follow my example, as I follow the example of Christ"; Philippians 3:17: "Join with others in following my example, brothers, and take note of those who live according to the pattern we gave you"; Philippians 4:9: "Whatever you have learned or received or heard from me, or seen in me—put it into practice"; 1 Thessalonians 1:6: "You became imitators of us and of the Lord"; 2 Thessalonians 3:7–9: "For you yourselves know how you ought to follow our example. We were not idle when we were with you, nor did we eat anyone's food without paying for it. On the contrary, we worked night and day, laboring and toiling so that we would not be a burden to any of you. We did this not because we do not have the right to such help, but in order to make ourselves a model for you to follow."

If Paul, as a model of prayer, is not as much studied or appealed to as he is in other respects, it is not because he is not a remarkable proof of what grace can do. Neither is it because we do not in this respect stand in need of the help of his example. A study of Paul as a model of prayer will bring a rich reward of instruction and encouragement.

The words our Lord used of him at his conversion, "He is praying," may be taken as the keynote of Paul's life. The heavenly vision that brought him to his knees ruled his life ever after. Christ at the right hand of God, in whom we are blessed with all spiritual blessings, was everything to Paul. Prayer and the expectation of heavenly power in his work and on his work was the simple outcome of Paul's faith in the Glorified One. In this too Christ meant him to be a model by whom we might learn that exactly in the measure in which the heavenliness of Christ and His gifts and the otherworldliness of the powers that work for salvation are known and believed will prayer become the spontaneous rising of the heart to the only source of its life.

Paul's Habits of Prayer

Paul reveals his prayer habits almost unconsciously. He writes in Romans 1:9–11: "God, whom I serve with my whole heart in preaching the gospel of his Son, is my witness how constantly I remember you in my prayers. I long to see you so that I may impart to you some spiritual gift to make you strong."

And in Romans 10:1; 9:2–3: "Brothers, my heart's desire and prayer to God for the Israelites is that they may be saved. I have great sorrow and unceasing anguish in my heart. For I could wish that I myself were cursed and cut off from Christ for the sake of my brothers."

"I always thank God for you because of his grace given you in Christ Jesus" (1 Corinthians 1:4).

"Rather, as servants of God we commend ourselves in every way: in great endurance; in troubles, hardships and distresses; in beatings, imprisonments and riots; in hard work, sleepless nights and hunger; in purity, understanding, patience and kindness; in the Holy Spirit and in sincere love" (2 Corinthians 6:4–6).

"My dear children, for whom I am again in the pains of childbirth until Christ is formed in you . . ." (Galatians 4:19).

"For this reason, ever since I heard about your faith in the Lord Jesus and your love for all the saints I have not stopped giving thanks for you, remembering you in my prayers. I keep asking that the God of our Lord Jesus Christ, the glorious Father, may give you the Spirit of wisdom and revelation, so that you may know him better. I pray also that the eyes of your heart may be enlightened in order that you may know the hope to which he has called you, the riches of his glorious inheritance in the saints" (Ephesians 1:14–18).

"For this reason I kneel before the Father, from whom his whole family in heaven and on earth derives its name. I pray that out of his glorious riches he may strengthen you with power through his Spirit in your inner being so that Christ may dwell in your hearts through faith. And I pray that you, being rooted and established in love, may have power, together with all the saints, to grasp how wide and long and high and deep is the love of Christ, and to know this love that surpasses knowledge—that you may be filled to the measure of all the fullness of God" (Ephesians 3:14–19).

"I thank my God every time I remember you. In all my prayers for all of you, I always pray with joy. God can testify how I long for all of you with the affection of Christ Jesus. And this is my prayer: that your love may abound more and more in knowledge and depth of insight so that you may be able to discern what is best and may be pure and blameless until the day of Christ, filled with the fruit of righteousness that comes through Jesus Christ—to the glory and praise of God" (Philippians 1:3–4, 8–11).

"We always thank God, the Father of our Lord Jesus Christ, when we pray for you. For this reason, since the day we heard about you, we have not stopped praying for you and asking God to fill you with the knowledge of his will through all spiritual wisdom and understanding. And we pray this in order that you may live a life worthy of the Lord and may please him in every way: bearing fruit in every good work, growing in the knowledge of God, being strengthened with all power according to his glorious might so that you may have great endurance and patience, and joyfully giving thanks to the Father, who has qualified you to share in the inheritance of the saints in the kingdom of light" (Colossians 1:3, 9–12).

"I want you to know how much I am struggling for you and for those at Laodicea, and for all who have not met me personally" (Colossians 2:1).

"We always thank God for all of you, mentioning you in our prayers" (1 Thessalonians 1:2).

"How can we thank God enough for you in return for all the joy we have in the presence of our God because of you? Night and day we pray most earnestly that we may see you again and supply what is lacking in your faith. May the Lord make your love increase and overflow for each other and for everyone else, just as ours does for you. May he strengthen your hearts so that you will be blameless and holy in the presence of our God and Father when our Lord Jesus comes with all his holy ones" (1 Thessalonians 3:9–10, 12–13).

"May God himself, the God of peace, sanctify you through and through. May your whole spirit, soul and body be kept blameless at the coming of our Lord Jesus Christ" (1 Thessalonians 5:23).

"We ought always to thank God for you, brothers, and rightly so, because your faith is growing more and more, and the love every one of you has for each other is increasing. With this in mind, we constantly pray for you, that our God may count you worthy of his calling, and that by his power he may fulfill every good purpose of yours and every act prompted by your faith" (2 Thessalonians 1:3, 11).

"I always thank my God as I remember you in my prayers" (Philemon 1:4).

"I thank God, whom I serve, as my forefathers did, with a clear conscience, as night and day I constantly remember you in my prayers" (2 Timothy 1:3).

These passages taken together give us the picture of a man whose words "Pray without ceasing" were simply the expression of his daily life. He had a great sense of the insufficiency of conversion without prayer for growth and grace. He saw the need of much and unceasing prayer, day and night, to bring down the Holy Spirit, and was so sure that prayer would bring Him down that his life was one of continual and specific prayer.

Paul had such a sense that everything must come from above, and such a faith that it would come in answer to prayer, that prayer was neither a duty nor a burden. It was the natural turning of the heart to the only place from where it could possibly obtain what it sought for others.

The Contents of Paul's Prayers

It is just as important to know *what* Paul prayed as to know how frequently and earnestly he did so. Intercession is a spiritual work. Our confidence in it will depend much on our knowing that we ask according to the will of God. The more distinctly we ask for spiritual things, which we know God alone can bestow, the more direct and urgent will be our appeal to God alone. The more impossible the things seem that we seek, the more we will turn from all human sources to prayer and to God alone.

In the epistles, in addition to expressions in which he speaks of his praying, we have a number of distinct prayers in which Paul expresses his heart's desire for those to whom he writes. In these we see that his first desire was always that they might be established in the Christian life. As much as he praised God when he heard of a conversion, he knew how weak the young converts were. He knew nothing would avail for their establishment in the faith but the grace and power of the Spirit. If we look at some of the main points of these prayers, we will see what he asked for and obtained.

Consider the two prayers in Ephesians—the one for light and the other for strength. In the former (1:15–18), he prays for the Spirit of wisdom to enlighten them to know their calling, their inheritance, and the mighty power of God working in them. Spiritual enlightenment and knowledge was their greatest need, obtained for them through prayer.

In the latter (3:14–19), he asks that the power they had been led to see in Christ might work in them. He asks that they be strengthened with divine might, so as to have the indwelling

Christ, the love that surpasses knowledge, and the fullness of God actually come on them. These were things that could only come directly from heaven; things for which he asked and expected. If we want to learn Paul's art of intercession, we must ask nothing less for believers in our day.

Look at the prayer in Philippians (1:9–11). There, too, it is first for spiritual knowledge, then a blameless life, and then a fruitful life to the glory of God. This is also true in the beautiful prayer in Colossians (1:9–12)—first, spiritual knowledge and understanding of God's will, then the strengthening with all might to all patience and joy.

Consider the two prayers in 1 Thessalonians 3:12–13 and 5:23. The one: "May the Lord make your love increase and overflow for each other and for everyone else just as ours does for you. May he strengthen your hearts so that you will be blameless and holy in the presence of our God." The other: "May God himself, the God of peace, sanctify you through and through. May your whole spirit, soul and body be kept blameless at the coming of our Lord Jesus Christ." The very words are so high that we hardly understand, much less believe and even less experience what they mean. Paul so lived in the heavenly world and was so at home in the holiness and omnipotence of God and His love that such prayers were the natural expression of what he knew God could and would do.

"May God himself . . . sanctify you through and through. May your whole spirit . . . be kept blameless and holy." The man who believes in these things and desires them will pray for them for others also. Paul's prayers are proof that he seeks for them the very life of heaven upon earth. No wonder he was not tempted to trust in any human means, but looked for it from heaven alone. I say again, the more we take Paul's prayers as our pattern, and make his desires our own for believers for whom we pray, the more will prayer become as our daily breath.

Paul's Requests for Prayer

Paul's requests are no less instructive than his own prayers for the saints. They show that he does not count prayer a special prerogative of an apostle; he invites the humblest and simplest believer to claim his right. They prove that he doesn't think only the new converts or weak Christians need prayer; he himself, as a member of the body, is dependent upon his brethren and their prayers.

After Paul had preached the Gospel for twenty years, he still asked for prayer that he might speak as he ought to speak. Not once for all, not for a time, but day by day and without ceasing, grace must be sought for the work. United, continued waiting on God was to Paul the only hope of the church. When the Holy Spirit came, the life of the Lord in heaven entered the world; nothing but unbroken communication with heaven can maintain it.

Listen how Paul asks for prayer, and with what urgency: Romans 15:30–32:

> I urge you, brothers, by our Lord Jesus Christ and by the love of the Spirit, to join me in my struggle by praying to God for me. Pray that I may be rescued from the unbelievers in Judea and that my service in Jerusalem may be

acceptable to the saints there, so that by God's will I may come to you with joy and together with you be refreshed.

How remarkably both prayers were answered: The Roman world-power that—in Pilate with Christ and in Herod with Peter at Philippi—had proved its antagonism to God's kingdom, suddenly becomes Paul's protector and secures him a safe convoy to Rome. This can only be accounted for because of these prayers.

Consider these other requests by Paul:

> He has delivered us from such a deadly peril, and he will deliver us. On him we have set our hope that he will continue to deliver us, as you help us by your prayers. Then many will give thanks on our behalf for the gracious favor granted us in answer to the prayers of many. (2 Corinthians 1:10–11)
>
> And pray in the Spirit on all occasions with all kinds of prayers and requests. With this in mind, be alert and always keep on praying for all the saints. Pray also for me, that whenever I open my mouth, words may be given me so that I will fearlessly make known the mystery of the gospel, for which I am an ambassador in chains. Pray that I may declare it fearlessly, as I should. (Ephesians 6:18–20)
>
> For I know that through your prayers and the help given by the Spirit of Jesus Christ, what has happened to me will turn out for my deliverance. (Philippians 1:19)
>
> Devote yourselves to prayer, being watchful and thankful. And pray for us, too, that God may open a door for our message, so that we may proclaim the mystery of Christ, for which I am in chains. Pray that I may proclaim it clearly, as I should. (Colossians 4:2–4)

Brothers, pray for us. (1 Thessalonians 5:25)

I hope to be restored to you in answer to your prayers. (Philemon 22)

We saw how Christ prayed and taught His disciples to pray. We see how Paul prayed and taught the churches to pray. As the Master called, so the servant calls us to believe and to prove that prayer is the power both of the ministry and of the church.

Paul's faith is summarized in these remarkable words concerning a situation that caused him grief: "This will turn to my salvation through your prayer and the supply of the Spirit of Jesus Christ." He depended upon his Lord and equally upon his brethren to secure the supply of that Spirit for him. The Spirit from heaven and prayer on earth were to Paul, as to the Twelve after Pentecost, inseparably linked. We speak often of apostolic zeal, devotion, and power. May God give us a revival of apostolic *prayer.*

Does the work of intercession take the place in the church it ought to have? Is it commonly understood in the Lord's work that everything depends upon getting from God that "supply of the Spirit of Christ" for ourselves that can give our work its power to bless? This is Christ's divine order for all ministry—His own and that of His servants. This is the pattern Paul followed: First, come every day empty-handed and receive from God the supply of the Spirit in intercession. Then impart what has come to you to others.

In all His instructions, our Lord Jesus spoke more frequently to His disciples about their praying than their preaching. In the farewell discourse, He said little about preaching but much about the Holy Spirit and about their asking whatever they would in His name.

If we are to taste of the life of the early apostles, including Paul, we must genuinely accept the truth that our first responsibility is intercession—to secure the power of God on the souls entrusted to us. We must first have the courage to confess our own sins and to believe that there is deliverance. Breaking old habits, resisting the clamor of pressing needs that have always had priority, making every other call subordinate to this one—whether others approve or not—will not be easy at first. But those who are faithful will not only have a reward themselves but they will become benefactors to those for whom they intercede.

Is it possible that those who have never been able to face much less overcome the difficulty still become mighty in prayer? Answer this: Was it possible for Jacob to become Israel—a prince who prevailed with God? The things that are impossible with men are possible with God. Have we not received from the Father, as the fruit of Christ's redemption, the Spirit of supplication and of intercession? Stop and think about what this means. Do you still doubt whether God is able to make you a "striver with God," a prince who prevails with Him?

We must cast aside all fear and in faith claim the grace for which we have the Holy Spirit dwelling in us—the grace of supplication and intercession. We must persistently believe that He lives in us and will enable us to do the work of prayer. We must in faith accept and yield ourselves to the truth that intercession as the great work of the King on the throne is also the great work of His servants on earth.

We have the Holy Spirit, who brings the Christ-life into our hearts to prepare us for this work. Let us begin to stir up the gift within us. As we set aside time each day for intercession, and count upon the Spirit's enabling power, confidence will grow that we can, in our own measure, follow Paul even as he followed Christ.

Chapter 14

God Seeks Intercessors

He saw that there was no one, he was appalled that there was no one to intervene; so his own arm worked salvation for him, and his own righteousness sustained him.

Isaiah 59:16

I have posted watchmen on your walls, O Jerusalem; they will never be silent day or night. You who call on the LORD, give yourselves no rest, and give him no rest till he establishes Jerusalem and makes her the praise of the earth.

Isaiah 62:6–7

I looked, but there was no one to help, I was appalled that no one gave support; so my own arm worked salvation for me, and my own wrath sustained me.

Isaiah 63:5

No one calls on your name or strives to lay hold of you; for you have hidden your face from us and made us waste away because of our sins.

Isaiah 64:7

"I looked for a man among them who would build up the wall and stand before me in the gap on behalf of the land so I would not have to destroy it, but I found none."

Ezekiel 22:30

"You did not choose me, but I chose you and appointed you to go and bear fruit—fruit that will last. Then the Father will give you whatever you ask in my name."

John 15:16

In the study of the star-studded heavens, much depends upon a clear understanding of relative sizes or magnitudes. Without some sense of the size of the heavenly bodies that appear so small to the naked eye and yet are so great, and of the almost infinite extent of the regions in which they move, though they appear so near and so familiar, there can be no true knowledge of the heavenly world or of its relation to this earth. It is the same with the spiritual heavens and the spiritual life we are called upon to live. It is especially so in the life of intercession, that wonderful interaction between heaven and earth. Everything depends upon the right understanding of magnitudes or relative importance in the spiritual realm.

Think of three elements first: There is the world with its needs, entirely dependent upon and waiting to be helped by intercession (knowing or unknowingly); there is God in heaven with His all-sufficient supply for all those needs, waiting to be asked; and there is the church (or the body of Christ) with its magnificent calling and its sure promises, waiting to be stirred to a sense of its awesome responsibility and power.

God seeks intercessors. There is a world out there with millions who are perishing without Christ. The work of intercession is its only hope. Much of our expressions of love and work in ministry are comparatively vain because there is so little real intercession connected with it. Millions live as though there never were such a one as the Son of God who died for them. Millions pass into outer darkness without hope year after year. Of the millions who bear the name of Christ the great majority live in utter ignorance or indifference.

What of the numberless weak, even sickly, Christians who could be blessed by intercession and used of God in it if they would but avail themselves of this privilege? Churches and mission organizations sacrifice lives and labor with little result only for lack of intercession. Every soul is worth more than the world, and nothing less than the price paid for them by Christ's blood. They are within reach of the power that can be tapped through intercession. We have no concept of the magnitude of the work to be done by God's intercessors or we would cry out to God for an outpouring of the spirit of intercession.

God is looking for intercessors. There is a God of glory able to meet all of our needs. We are told that He delights in mercy, that He waits to be gracious, that He longs to pour out His blessing. The love that gave the Son over to death is the measure of the love that each moment surrounds every human being. But still they perish, millions each year. It seems that God does not move to save them.

If God does so love and long to bless, there must be some inscrutable reason for His holding back. What is it? The Scripture uses a telling phrase: "Because of your unbelief." God's apparent lack of moving is directly connected to the faithlessness of God's people. He has taken them into partnership with himself; He has honored them and bound himself to them by making their prayers a standard against which to measure the working of His power to save souls.

A lack of intercession is one of the primary causes of lack of blessing. Oh, that we would turn eyes and heart from everything else and fix them upon the God who hears our prayers until the magnificence of His promises and His power and His purpose of love overwhelm us!

God works through intercessors. There is a third magnitude to which our eyes must be opened: the stupendous privilege and power of intercessors. There is a false humility that makes self-depreciation a virtue—because those who claim it have never seen their utter nothingness. If they realized it, they would not apologize for weakness but glory in it as the one condition of Christ's power resting on them. A true grasp of the intercessor's power source would cause that one to judge his power and influence before God in prayer as little by what it sees or feels as we judge the size of the sun or stars by what we can see with the naked eye.

Faith sees man as created in God's image and likeness to be God's representative in this world and have dominion over it. Faith sees man redeemed and in union with Christ, abiding in Him, identified with Him, and clothed with His power in intercession. Faith sees the Holy Spirit dwelling in us and praying through our sighs and groans, making intercession before God. Faith sees the intercession of the saints as part of the life of the Holy Trinity: the believer as God's child asking of the Father, in the Son, through the Spirit. Faith sees something of the divine appropriateness and beauty of this plan of salvation wrought through intercession and awakens the soul to an awareness of its amazing and wonderful calling.

God honors intercessors. When God called His people out of Egypt, He separated the priestly tribe to draw near to Him, stand before Him, and bless the people in His name. From time to time He sought, found, and especially honored intercessors, for whose sake He spared or blessed His people. When our Lord left the earth, He said to the inner circle He had gathered around Him, those with a special devotion to His service (which access is still available to every follower of Christ): "You did not choose me, but I chose you and appointed you to go and bear fruit—fruit that will last. Then the Father will give you whatever you ask in my name."

We have already pointed out that the three wonderful words "whatever you ask" were repeated six times. In them Christ placed the powers of the heavenly world at the disciples' disposal—not for their own selfish use but for the growth of His kingdom. We know from the record how wonderfully they used this power. Down through the ages the apostles have had their successors, men who have proved how God works in answer to prayer.

We may praise God that in our day too there is an ever-increasing number who are beginning to see and prove that in the church and in missions, in large organizations as well as small groups and individual effort, intercession is being acknowledged as the primary power by which God moves and opens heaven. They are learning, and long to teach others. Those who in the power of the Holy Spirit have received from heaven what they communicate to others will be best able to do the Lord's work.

God waits for intercessors. God had His appointed servants in Israel—watchmen He chose to cry to Him day and night and give Him no rest. Yet He often had to wonder that there was no intercessor, no one willing to stir himself up to take hold of God's strength.

In our day He still waits and wonders that there are not more intercessors, that all His children do not give themselves to this high and holy work. He is saddened that those who do intercede do not engage in it more intensely and with greater perseverance. He wonders at ministers of the Gospel who complain that their duties do not allow them time for intercession, which should be their first, their highest, their most delightful work, and which is alone effective for winning souls. He wonders at His children who have forsaken home and friends and lands for His sake and the Gospel's, and yet fall short in what He intended to be their abiding strength: receiving daily all they need to impart to those who walk in darkness. He wonders at the multitudes of His children who have hardly any concept of what intercession is. He wonders further at the multitudes more that have learned it is their duty and seek to obey it, but confess that they know but little of the actual laying hold upon God or prevailing with Him.

God longs to answer the true intercessor. God desires to dispense larger blessings. He longs to reveal His power and glory as God and to show His saving love more abundantly. He seeks intercessors in larger numbers and greater power to prepare the way of the Lord. Where can He find them but in His church? He has entrusted to His church the task of telling its people of their Lord's need, the task of encouraging and training and preparing them for His holy service.

In His Word God speaks of widows who trust in God and continue in supplication night and day. There are many in the church who are beyond the age of active service in other areas, but who could serve mightily in the place of intercession.

God looks also to the great host of young people who have given themselves in solemn pledges to obey the Lord Jesus Christ at all cost, and wonders how many are being trained to go beyond the service of the weekly prayer meeting and find their place in strong intercessory prayer for souls.

Ministers and missionaries alike must understand their opportunity to train the believers of their congregations to be those who by prayer find the lost sheep and bring them into the fold.

God will not take this work out of the hands of His church. For this reason, He comes to us in various ways and by various means to convince us of the great need. It may be through someone whom He raises up to live a life of faith in His service and thus proves how surely and abundantly He answers prayer; another may be through the story of a church that makes prayer for souls its focal point and bears testimony to God's faithfulness; a missionary work in a distant country can show how special prayer in unique situations can meet extreme physical and spiritual need where the powers of this world and Satan's realm have long held sway. Perhaps a season of revival may come in answer to united urgent supplication by God's people in a church otherwise unknown and unremarkable. In these and many other ways God shows us what intercession can do. He pleads with us to wake up and train His great host of followers to be a people of intercession.

God seeks intercessors. God sends His servants out to find them. Let ministers and pastors make this a part of their responsibility. Let them make their church a training school for intercession. Give the people specific objectives for prayer. Encourage them to set aside a definite time for it even if it is only ten minutes each day. Help them to understand the boldness they can have with God. Teach them to expect and look for answers. Show them what it is to first pray and get an answer in private, and then to take the answer and scatter the blessing to others. Tell everyone who is master of his own time that he is as free as the angels to wait before the throne and then to go out and minister life to the heirs of salvation. Spread the news that this honor is for all of God's people. There is no discrimination. A domestic servant, a physical laborer, a bedridden individual, a daughter living in her mother's home, a young man in business—all are called to pray, and everyone is needed.

Where are the intercessors? As ministers of the Gospel take up the challenge of finding and training intercessors, it will no doubt move them to pray more. Christ gave Paul as a pattern of His grace before He made him a preacher of it. It has been well said, "The first duty of a clergyman is to humbly pray that all he would have God do in his people may first be done in himself."

The effort to bring this message of God may cause much heart-searching and even humiliation. But the best practice for doing anything is teaching others to do it.

Servants of Christ, set as watchmen to cry unto God day and night, let us awake to our holy calling. Let us believe in the power of intercessory prayer. Let us practice it. Giving our time and efforts to God in intercession will promote this same spirit in those we teach and for whom we pray.

Chapter 15

The Coming Revival

Will you not revive us again, that your people may rejoice in you?

Psalm 85:6

*LORD, I have heard of your fame; I stand in awe of your deeds,
O LORD. Renew them in our day, in our time make them known;
in wrath remember mercy.*

Habakkuk 3:2

*"I live in a high and holy place, but also with him who is contrite and
lowly in spirit, to revive the spirit of the lowly and to revive the
heart of the contrite."*

Isaiah 57:15

*"Come, let us return to the LORD. He has torn us to pieces but he will
heal us; he has injured us but he will bind up our wounds. After two days
he will revive us; on the third day he will restore us, that we may live
in his presence."*

Hosea 6:1–2

"Revival is coming!" We may frequently hear the comment. There
are many teachers who see the signs of its approach and confidently herald its soon appearance. The increase of interest in mis-

sions, the news of revivals in places where all was dead or cold; the hosts of young people gathered together in retreat or outreach; the open doors everywhere in the Christian and the pagan world; the victories already won in the fields white unto the harvest, wherever believing, hopeful workers enter—all strengthen the assurance of a time of power and blessing to come such as we have never known. The church is about to enter into a new era of increasing spirituality and greater extension.

There are others who, while admitting the truth of some of these facts, still fear that the conclusions drawn from them are one-sided and premature. They see the interest in missions increased but point at the small circle to which it is confined, and how utterly out of proportion it is to what it ought to be.

To the great majority of church members and to the greater part of the church as a whole, the issue is as yet anything but a vital question. They point to the power of worldliness and materialism, of the increase of a money-making, pleasure-loving spirit among professing Christians, of the lack of spirituality in many of our churches, and the continuing and apparently increasing estrangement of multitudes from the Lord's Day and His Word as proof that the great revival has certainly not begun and is hardly thought of by most. They say that they do not see the deep humiliation, the intense desire, the fervent prayer, which appear as forerunners of every true revival.

There are right-hand and left-hand errors that are equally dangerous. We must seek as much to be kept from superficial optimism, which is not able to gauge the extent of evil, as from hopeless pessimism, which can neither praise God for what He has done nor trust Him for what He is ready to do. The former will lose itself in a congratulation of self that rejoices in its zeal and diligence and apparent success. It never sees the need of confession and striving in prayer that is needed before we are prepared to meet and conquer the hosts of darkness. The latter virtually gives the world over to Satan and almost rejoices to see things get worse, thinking to hasten the coming of Him who is to put everything right.

May God keep us from both errors and fulfill the promise "Whether you turn to the right or to the left, your ears will hear a voice behind you, saying, 'This is the way; walk in it'" (Isaiah 30:21). Let us listen to the lessons suggested by our opening texts; they may help us to pray the prayer: "Revive your work, O Lord!"

1. *Revive your work, O Lord!* See how all our texts contain the one thought: Revival is God's work, He alone can give it; it must come from above. We are frequently in danger of looking to what God has done and is doing and to count on that as the pledge that He will immediately do more. Yet He may be blessing us up to the measure of our faith or self-sacrifice and cannot give a larger measure until there has been a new discovery and confession of what is hindering Him. We also may be looking to all the signs of life and good around us, and congratulating ourselves on all the organizations and support groups that are being created, while the need of God's direct intervention is not significantly felt and entire dependence upon Him is not cultivated.

Regeneration, the giving of divine life, we all acknowledge to be God's act, a miracle of His power. The restoring or reviving of the divine life in a soul or a church is equally a supernatural work. To have the spiritual discernment that understands the signs of the heavens and can foretell the coming of revival, we need to enter deeply into God's mind and will as to its conditions and the preparedness of those who pray for it or who are to be used to bring it about. Surely the Lord God will do nothing except reveal His secrets unto His servants. It is God who gives revival; it is absolute dependence upon God, giving Him the honor and the glory, that will prepare us for it.

2. *Revive us in answer to prayer.* A second lesson suggested is that the revival God is to give will be given in answer to prayer. It must be asked for and received from God himself.

Those who know anything of the history of revivals will remember how often this has been proven—both widespread and local revivals have been distinctly traced to specific prayer. In our own day there are numbers of congregations and mission groups where special or ongoing revivals are—all glory be to God—connected with systematic, believing prayer. The coming revival will be no exception. An extraordinary spirit of prayer, urging believers to private as well as united prayer, motivating them to labor fervently in their supplications, will be one of the surest signs of approaching showers and floods of blessing.

Let all who are burdened with a lack of spirituality or with the mediocre state of the life of God in believers, listen to the call that comes to us all: If there is to be revival—a true, divine outpouring of God's Spirit—it will correspond with wholehearted prayer and faith.

No believer should think that he or she is too weak to help, or imagine that his or her input would not be missed. If we but begin, the gift that is in us will be so evident that we will become God's chosen intercessor for our own circle of friends or neighborhood.

Think of the need of souls, of all the sins and shortcomings among God's people, of the lack of power in so many of our sermons. Then begin to cry to God, "Will you not revive us again that your people may rejoice in you?" Let us press the truth deep in our hearts: Every revival comes, as Pentecost came, as a direct result of united and continued prayer. So the coming revival must begin with a great revival of prayer. It is in the prayer closet, with the door shut, that the sound of abundance of rain will first be heard. An increase of private prayer among ministers and laypeople will be a sure indication of coming blessing.

3. *Revive us in answer to the prayer of the humble and contrite.* A third lesson our texts teach is that revival is promised to the humble and contrite. We want revival to come upon the proud and the self-satisfied, to break them down and save them. God will do this, but only on the condition that those who see and feel the sin of others take their burden and bear it before the Lord.

All those who pray for and claim in faith God's reviving power for His church must humble themselves with a confession of sins. Need of revival always points to previous decline, and decline is always caused by sin. Humiliation and contrition have always been the conditions for revival. In all intercession, confession of man's sin and declaration of God's righteous judgment are essential elements.

This pattern can be traced throughout the history of Israel. It is demonstrated in the reformations under the pious kings of Judah. We hear it in the prayers of men like Ezra, Nehemiah, and Daniel. In Isaiah, Jeremiah, and Ezekiel, as well as in the Minor Prophets, it is the keynote of warning as well as of promise. If there is no humbling of God's people and forsaking of sin, there can be no revival or deliverance. When men have set up idols in their hearts, they are not apt to inquire of God. But when a man is of a poor and contrite spirit, he trembles at the Word of God and before His Spirit. Amid the most gracious promises of divine visitation, there is added this note: "Be ashamed and confounded for your own ways, O house of Israel."

We find the same emphasis in the New Testament. The Sermon on the Mount promises the kingdom to the poor and to those who mourn. In the epistles to the Corinthians and the Galatians, the religion of man—worldly wisdom and confidence in the flesh—is exposed and denounced; without its being confessed and forsaken, all the promises of grace and of the Spirit will be in vain.

The letters to the seven churches show us five churches of which God, out of whose mouth goes the sharp, two-edged sword, says He has something against them. In each of these the keyword of His message is not to the unconverted but to the church: "Repent!" All the glorious promises each of these letters contain share one condition, right down to the invitation, "Open the door and I will come in," and the promise, "He that overcomes will sit with me on my throne." All are dependent on the one word: "Repent!"

If there is to be a revival—not among the unsaved but in our churches—that word must be heard. Was it only in Israel in the ministry of the kings and the prophets that there was so much evil to be cleansed away? Was it only in the church of the first century that Paul and James and our Lord himself had to speak such sharp words?

Is there not in the church of our day an idolatry of money and talent and culture—unfaithfulness to its one husband and Lord, and a confidence in the flesh that grieves and resists God's Holy Spirit? And is there not a common confession of a lack of spirituality and spiritual power?

Let all who long for coming revival and who seek to hasten it by their prayers, pray this above everything, that the Lord may prepare His prophets to go before Him at His bidding: "Cry aloud, spare not, lift up your voice like a trumpet, and show my people their transgression."

Every true revival among God's people must have at its roots a deep sense and confession of sin. Until those who would lead the church in the path of revival bear faithful testimony against the sins of the church, it is likely that it will find people unprepared. Most would prefer to have a revival as the result of their programs and efforts. God's way is the opposite. Out of death, acknowledged as the wage of sin, and confession of utter helplessness, God revives.

4. *Revive us as we return to you.* There is a final thought, suggested by the text from Hosea. It is as we return to the Lord that revival will come; for if we had not wandered from Him, His life would still be among us in power. "Come, let us return to the Lord. He has torn us to pieces but he will heal us; he has injured us but he will bind up our wounds. After two days he will revive us; on the third day he will restore us, that we may live in his presence."

As we have said, where there is no sense or confession of waywardness, there can be no returning to the Lord. *Let us return to the Lord* must be the watchword of revival. Let us return, acknowledging and forsaking whatever there has been in the church that is not entirely according to His mind and Spirit. Let us return and turn over and cast out whatever there has been in our walk of the power of God's two great enemies: confidence in the flesh, or the spirit of the world. In the acknowledgement of how undividedly God must have us in order to fill us with His Spirit and use us for the kingdom of His Son, let us return to Him. Return in the surrender of a dependence and a devotion that has no measure but the absolute claim of Him who is the Lord! With our whole heart, let us come back, asking that He may make and keep us wholly His. He will revive us, and we will live in His sight. Let us turn to the God of Pentecost, as Christ led His disciples to turn to Him, and the God of Pentecost will turn to us.

It is for this returning to the Lord that the great work of intercession is needed. Here the coming revival must find its strength. Let us begin as individuals to plead in secret with God, confessing whatever we see of sin or hindrance in ourselves. If there were not one other sin, surely our lack of prayer is reason enough for repentance and confession and returning to the Lord.

Let us seek to foster the spirit of confession and supplication and intercession in those around us; help to encourage and to train those who think themselves too weak; and lift up our voice to proclaim the great truths. Revival must come from above. Revival must be received in faith but brought down by prayer. Revival comes to the humble and the contrite, and they in turn will carry it to others.

If we return to the Lord with our whole heart, He will revive us. On those who see these truths rests the solemn responsibility of yielding themselves to share and to carry out these requirements.

As each of us pleads for revival throughout the church, let us also cry to God for our own neighborhood or sphere of work. Let there be great searching in the heart of every minister and layworker as to whether they are ready to give such time and strength to prayer as God would have. Just as in public they are leaders of their larger or smaller circles, let them in secret take their places in the front rank of the great intercessory host. They must prevail with God before revival and floods of blessing can come. Of all who speak of, think of, or long for revival, let not one hold back in this great work of honest, earnest, specific pleading: Revive your work, O Lord! Will you not revive us again?

Come and return to the Lord. He will revive us! Let us follow on to know the Lord. His going forth is prepared as the morning; and he will come unto us as the rain, as the latter and former rain, on the earth. Amen. So be it.

Pray Without Ceasing

A Thirty-One-Day Course

Helps to Intercessory Prayer

"And pray in the Spirit on all occasions with all kinds of prayers and requests. With this in mind, be alert and always keep on praying for all the saints. Pray also for me, that whenever I open my mouth, words may be given me so that I will fearlessly make known the mystery of the gospel" (Ephesians 6:18–19).

"I urge, then, first of all, that requests, prayers, intercession and thanksgiving be made for everyone—for kings and all those in authority, that we may live peaceful and quiet lives in all godliness and holiness. This is good, and pleases God our Savior, who wants all men to be saved and to come to a knowledge of the truth" (1 Timothy 2:1–3).

"Therefore confess your sins to each other and pray for each other so that you may be healed. The prayer of a righteous man is powerful and effective" (James 5:16).

Pray without ceasing. Who can do this? How can one do it who is surrounded by the cares of daily life? How can a mother love her child without ceasing? How can the eyelid without ceasing protect the eye? How can I breathe and feel and hear without ceasing? Because all of these are functions of a normal healthy life. If the spiritual life is healthy, under the full power of the Holy Spirit, praying without ceasing will come naturally.

Does praying without ceasing refer to continual physical acts of prayer, in which we persevere until we obtain what we ask, or does it refer to the spirit of prayerfulness that animates and motivates us throughout the day? It includes both. The example of our Lord Jesus shows us this. We should enter our place of private prayer for special seasons of prayer, and we are at times to persevere there in importunate prayer. We are also to walk all day in God's presence, with our whole heart focused on spiritual things. Without set times of prayer, the spirit of prayer will be lacking and weak. Without the continual attitude of prayerfulness, the set times of prayer will be ineffective.

Does this running prayer refer only to prayer for ourselves, or for others? Both. It is only because many confine prayer to themselves that they fail to practice it correctly. It is only when the branch gives itself to bearing fruit that it lives a healthy life and can expect a rich flow of sap. The death of Christ brought Him to the place of everlasting intercession. Your death with Him to sin and self sets you free from the care of self and elevates you to the dignity of intercessor—one who can receive life and blessing from God for others. Know your calling; begin your work. Give yourself wholly to it, and soon you will find something of this "prayer without ceasing" within you.

How can we learn it? The best way to learn anything is simply to do it. Begin by setting apart some time every day, even ten or fifteen minutes, in which you say to God that you have come to Him as an intercessor for others. If you cannot keep the same time every day for prayer, do not let this trouble you. Only see that you do it. Christ chose you and appointed you to pray for others.

If at first you do not feel any special urgency or faith or power in your prayers, do not let that hinder you either. Quietly tell the Lord your thoughts; believe that the Holy Spirit is in you to teach you to pray; be assured that if you begin, God will help you. God cannot help you unless you begin and keep at it.

How do I know what to pray for? Once you begin, you will think of all the needs around you, and you will soon find enough to pray for. But to help you, this section was written with subjects and suggestions for prayer for one month. It is intended to be used month by month until we know more fully how to follow the Spirit's leading, and to make our own lists of subjects, and then to dispense with it. In regard to the use of these helps, I offer a few words of instruction.

1. *How to pray.* You will notice for each day there are two headings: "What to Pray" and "How to Pray." If actual subjects were given, one might fall into the routine of mentioning only names and things before God, and the work could become a burden. The suggestions under the heading "How to Pray" are meant to remind us of the spiritual nature of the work and of our need for divine help. They will encourage faith in the fact that God, through His Spirit, will give us grace to pray aright and will also hear our prayer. One does not all at once learn to take his place boldly and to dare to believe that he will be heard.

Take a few moments each day to listen to God's voice reminding you of how certainly even you will be heard and calling you to pray in that faith in your Father, to claim and take the blessings you have pleaded for. Let these words about how to pray enter your hearts and occupy your thoughts at other times too. The work of intercession is Christ's great work on earth, entrusted to Him because He gave himself as a sacrifice to God for men. The work of intercession is the greatest work a Christian can do. Give yourself as a sacrifice to God for men, and the work will become your greatest joy.

2. *What to pray.* Scripture calls us to pray for many things: for all saints, for all people, for kings and rulers, for all who are in adversity, for the sending forth of laborers, for those who labor in the Gospel, for all converts, for believers who have fallen into sin, and for one another in our own immediate circles. The church is now so much larger than when the New Testament was written; the number of forms of work and workers is so much greater; the needs of the church and the world are so much better known, that we need to take time and thought to see where prayer is needed and to what our heart is most drawn.

The scriptural calls to prayer demand a large heart that takes in the saints, the wayward, and every need. An attempt has been made in these helps to indicate the primary subjects that need prayer and that ought to interest every Christian.

It will seem difficult for many to pray for such large spheres as are sometimes mentioned. Let it be understood that in each case we may make special intercession for our own circle of interest coming under that heading. And it is hardly necessary to say that where one subject appears of greater interest or urgency than another, we are free for a time, day after day, to take up that subject. If time is truly given to intercession, and the spirit of believing prayer is cultivated, the object will be attained. While on the one hand the heart must be enlarged at times to take in all that needs prayer, the more direct and individualized our prayer, the better. Add your own list of further requests as you see fit.

3. *Answers to prayer.* More than one book has been published in which Christians may keep a register of their petitions and note when they were answered. This book does not provide that format. When we pray for other Christians or for particular ministries, it is difficult to know when or how our prayer is answered, or whether our prayer has had any part in bringing the answer. But it is of extreme importance that we prove to ourselves that God hears us, and to this end take note of what answers we are looking for and when they do come. On the day of praying for all saints, take those in your congregation or in your prayer meeting or Bible study group, and ask for a revival among them. In connection with missions, think of a particular missionary or even a country or people group that you are interested in, or more than one, and plead for God's blessing in the life of that missionary and those he ministers to and for a particular people group who need the Gospel preached to them. Expect and look for answers that you may praise God for them.

4. *Prayer groups.* There is no desire in publishing this invitation to intercession to add another to the many existing prayer groups or circles that meet regularly. The first objective is to stir the many Christians who—through ignorance of their calling or unbelief as to their prayers' effectiveness—are inactive when it comes to intercession; and then to help those who do pray to some fuller apprehension of the greatness of the work and the need of giving all their strength to it.

There is a prayer circle that asks for prayer on the first day of every month for the fuller manifestation of the power of the Holy Spirit throughout the church. I have made the words of that invitation the subject for the first day and taken the same thought as keynote throughout. The more one thinks of the need and the promise, and the greatness of the obstacles to be overcome in prayer, the more one feels it must become our life's work day by day, to which every other interest is subordinated.

But while not forming a large prayer group, it is suggested that it may be found helpful to have small prayer circles to unite in prayer either for one month, with some special object introduced daily along with the others, or through a year or longer with the idea of strengthening one another in the ministry of intercession. If a minister were to invite some of his neighboring brothers and sisters to join in some of the special requests along with the printed agenda for supplication, or some of the more earnest members of his congregation to unite in prayer for revival, some of these might be trained to take his place in the great work of intercession, who may now stand idly by because no one has asked them to join in.

5. *Who is sufficient for these things?* The more we study about it and try to practice this ministry of intercessory prayer, the more we become overwhelmed by its greatness and our own weakness. Let every such impression remind us: "My grace is sufficient for you," and to answer truthfully, "Our sufficiency is of God" (2 Corinthians 3:5 KJV).

Take courage; it is in the intercession of Christ that you are called to take part. The burden and the agony, the triumph and the victory, are all His. Learn from Him, yield to His Spirit in you to know how to pray. He gave himself as a sacrifice to God for men that He might have the right and power of intercession. He bore the sin of many and made intercession for the transgressors.

Let your faith rest boldly on His finished work. Let your heart wholly identify itself with Him in His death and His life. Like Him, give yourself to God as a sacrifice for others. It is your highest privilege, it is your true and full union with Him; it will be to you, as to Him, your power for intercessory prayer.

Come and give your whole heart and life to this kind of prayer, and you will know its blessedness and its power. God asks nothing less; the world needs nothing less; let us offer to God what we have.

DAY ONE

What to Pray: For the Power of the Holy Spirit

"I pray that out of his glorious riches he may strengthen you with power through his Spirit in your inner being" (Ephesians 3:16).

"Do not leave Jerusalem, but wait for the gift my Father promised, which you have heard me speak about. For John baptized with water, but in a few days you will be baptized with the Holy Spirit" (Acts 1:4).

Pray for the fuller manifestation of the grace and energy of the blessed Spirit of God in the removal of all that is contrary to God's revealed will, so that we might not grieve the Holy Spirit but that He may work in greater power in the church for the exaltation of Christ and the blessing of souls.

God has one promise to and through His exalted Son. Our Lord has one gift to His church. The church has one need. All prayer unites in one petition: for the power of the Holy Spirit. Make it your one prayer.

How to Pray: As a Child Asks a Father

"Which of you fathers, if your son asks for a fish, will give him a snake instead? Or if he asks for an egg, will give him a scorpion? If you then, though you are evil, know how to give good gifts to your children, how much more will your Father in heaven give the Holy Spirit to those who ask him!" (Luke 11:11–13).

Ask as simply and trustfully as a child asks for bread. You can do this because God has sent the Spirit of His Son into your heart, crying, "Abba, Father." This Spirit is in you to give you childlike confidence. Believing that He is praying in you, ask for the power of the Holy Spirit to be with you everywhere. Mention particular places or groups where you especially desire His power to be manifest.

Your Own Prayer Requests

DAY TWO
What to Pray: For the Spirit of Supplication

"In the same way, the Spirit helps us in our weakness. We do not know what we ought to pray for, but the Spirit himself intercedes for us with groans that words cannot express" (Romans 8:26).

"And I will pour out on the house of David and the inhabitants of Jerusalem a spirit of grace and supplication" (Zechariah 12:10).

The evangelization of the world depends first of all upon a revival of prayer. Our greatest need—in spite of what we may imagine—is the need for the forgotten secret of prevailing, all-encompassing prayer.

Every child of God has the Holy Spirit within him to enable him to pray effectively. God waits to give a full measure of the Spirit, an added boost to our private and corporate prayer life. Ask for yourself and for all who would join you for the outpouring of the Spirit of supplication.

How to Pray: In the Spirit

"And pray in the Spirit on all occasions with all kinds of prayers and requests. With this in mind, be alert and always keep on praying for all the saints" (Ephesians 6:18).

"But you, dear friends, build yourselves up in your most holy faith and pray in the Holy Spirit" (Jude 20).

On the day of His resurrection, our Lord gave His disciples the Holy Spirit to enable them to wait for the full outpouring of the Spirit on the day of Pentecost. It is only in the power of the Spirit already in us, acknowledged and yielded to, that we can pray for His fuller manifestation. Tell the Father that it is the Spirit of His Son in you who is urging you to plead the promises.

Your Own Prayer Requests

DAY THREE

What to Pray: For All the Saints

"And pray in the Spirit on all occasions with all kinds of prayers and requests. With this in mind, be alert and always keep on praying for all the saints" (Ephesians 6:18).

Every member of a body is interested in the welfare of the whole body and exists to help and complete the others. Believers are one body and ought to pray not so much for the welfare of their own church or group but for all the saints. This large, unselfish attitude is proof that Christ's Spirit is teaching them to pray. Pray first for all believers and then for all those around you.

How to Pray: In the Love of the Spirit

"By this all men will know that you are my disciples, if you love one another" (John 13:35).

"That all of them may be one, Father, just as you are in me and I am in you. May they also be in us so that the world may believe that you have sent me" (John 17:21).

"I urge you, brothers, by our Lord Jesus Christ and by the love of the Spirit, to join me in my struggle by praying to God for me" (Romans 15:30).

"Above all, love each other deeply, because love covers over a multitude of sins" (1 Peter 4:8).

If we are to pray, we must love those for whom we pray. Let us resolve to love all people, and especially every child of

God. Let us pray in the fervency of this love, the love of the Spirit.

Your Own Prayer Requests

DAY FOUR
What to Pray: For the Spirit of Holiness

God is the Holy One. His people are a holy people. He says, "I am holy; I am the Lord that makes you holy." Christ prayed, "Sanctify them. Make them holy through your truth." Paul prayed, "May God establish your hearts unblameable in holiness" and "God sanctify you wholly."

Pray for all saints—God's holy ones—throughout the church that the Spirit of holiness may guide and direct them. Especially pray for new converts. Pray for the Christians in your own neighborhood or in your congregation. Pray for any you are especially close to. Think of their special needs, weaknesses, or sins, and pray that God will make them holy.

How to Pray: Trusting in God's Omnipotence

Things that are impossible with men are possible with God. Think of the things we ask for, some of which we think have little likelihood of coming to pass or being granted us. We think of our own insignificance, our own unworthiness. Why would God answer our prayer? <u>Prayer is not only wishing, or even asking, but believing and accepting.</u> <u>Be still before God and ask Him that you might know Him as the Almighty One.</u> Leave your petitions with Him who does the impossible.

Your Own Prayer Requests

DAY FIVE

What to Pray: That God's People Might Be Kept From the World

"I will remain in the world no longer, but they are still in the world, and I am coming to you. Holy Father, protect them by the power of your name—the name you gave me—so that they may be one as we are one. My prayer is not that you take them out of the world but that you protect them from the evil one. They are not of the world, even as I am not of it" (John 17:11, 15–16).

On His last night on earth, Christ asked three things for His disciples: that they might be kept as those who are not of the world; that they might be sanctified; that they might be one in love. You cannot do better than pray as Jesus prayed. Ask for God's people that they may be kept separate from the world and its spirit; that they, by the Holy Spirit, may live as one in love and as those who are not of the world.

How to Pray: Having Confidence Before God

"Dear friends, if our hearts do not condemn us, we have confidence before God and receive from him anything we ask, because we obey his commands and do what pleases him" (1 John 3:21–22).

Memorize these words. Get them into your heart. Join the ranks of those who with John draw near to God with an assured heart that does not condemn, having confidence toward God. In this spirit pray for your brother who sins (1 John 5:16). In the quiet confidence of an obedient child, plead for those of your brethren who may be giving in to sin. Pray for all to be kept from evil. And say often, "What we ask, we receive, because we keep His commandments and do what is right in His sight."

Your Own Prayer Requests

DAY SIX

What to Pray: For the Spirit of Love in the Church

"I have given them the glory that you gave me, that they may be one as we are one: I in them and you in me. May they be brought to complete unity to let the world know that you sent me and have loved them even as you have loved me. I have made you known to them and will continue to make you known in order that the love you have for me may be in them and that I myself may be in them" (John 17:22–23, 26).

"But the fruit of the Spirit is love" (Galatians 5:22).

Believers are one in Christ as He is one with the Father. The love of God rests on them and will dwell in them. Pray that the power of the Holy Spirit may so work this love in believers that the world may see it and know God's love for them. Let this be a continual subject of prayer.

How to Pray: As One of God's Reminders

"I have posted watchmen on your walls, O Jerusalem; they will never be silent day or night. You who call on the LORD, give yourselves no rest" (Isaiah 62:6).

Study these words until your soul is filled with the realization: I am appointed to be an intercessor. Enter God's presence in that conviction. Study the world's need with the thought: It is my work to intercede; the Holy Spirit will teach me what I am to pray for and how I am to pray. Let it be an abiding recognition: My great life work, like Christ's, is intercessory prayer—to pray for believers as well as for those who do not yet know God.

Your Own Prayer Requests

* Eric Paoli
* Mathew Lemieux
* Ryan Gilmaer
* Emily Somors
* Amy Kronzer
* Ralph Patterson

DAY SEVEN

What to Pray: For the Power of the Holy Spirit on His Ministers

"I urge you, brothers, by our Lord Jesus Christ and by the love of the Spirit, to join me in my struggle by praying to God for me" (Romans 15:30).

"He has delivered us from such a deadly peril, and he will deliver us. On him we have set our hope that he will continue to deliver us, as you help us by your prayers" (2 Corinthians 1:10–11).

What a great number of ministers there are in Christ's church. And what a need they have for prayer. What strength they might work in if they were all clothed with the power of the Holy Spirit. Pray for this, long and often. Think of your own pastor, and ask especially for him. Connect every ministry in your town or neighborhood or the world with the prayer that all might be filled with the Holy Spirit. Plead for them the promise that they will be clothed with power from on high.

How to Pray: In Secret

"But when you pray, go into your room, close the door and pray to your Father, who is unseen. Then your Father, who sees what is done in secret, will reward you" (Matthew 6:6).

"After he had dismissed them, he went up on a mountainside by himself to pray. When evening came, he was there alone. Jesus, knowing that they intended to come and make him king by force, withdrew again to a mountain by himself" (Matthew 14:23; John 6:15).

Take time to realize when you are alone with God: Here am I, face-to-face with God, to intercede for His servants. Never think you have no influence or that your prayer would not be missed. Your prayer and your faith will make a difference. Pray in secret to God for His ministers of the Gospel.

Your Own Prayer Requests

DAY EIGHT

What to Pray: For the Spirit on All Christian Workers

"On him we have set our hope that he will continue to deliver us, as you help us by your prayers. Then many will give thanks on our behalf for the gracious favor granted us in answer to the prayers of many" (2 Corinthians 1:11).

There are Christian workers in every walk of life: not only in our churches and missions but also in our schools, our hospitals, our government, our military, our highways, our farms, our markets, in business, and in leisure. God be praised for this! But think what more they could accomplish if each were living in the fullness of the Holy Spirit! Pray for them; it makes you a partner in their work, and you will have reason to praise God when you hear of blessing in their lives and in their work on every front.

How to Pray: With Specific Petitions

"What do you want me to do for you?" (Luke 18:41).

In the above reference, the Lord knew what the blind man wanted and yet He asked him. Verbalizing our desires gives credence to the transaction in which we are engaged with God and so awakens faith and expectation. Be specific in your petitions so as to know what answer you may look for. Think of the great number of Christians you know who are working for God in their various fields and endeavors, and ask and expect God to bless them and prosper them in answer to the prayers of His people. Ask even more specifically for those in your own family and place of work. Intercession is not the breathing out of pious wishes; it is believing, persevering prayer to receive specific answers to specific requests.

Your Own Prayer Requests

DAY NINE
What to Pray: For God's Spirit on Our Mission Fields

"While they were worshiping the Lord and fasting, the Holy Spirit said, 'Set apart for me Barnabas and Saul for the work to which I have called them.' So after they had fasted and prayed, they placed their hands on them and sent them off. The two of them, sent on their way by the Holy Spirit, went down to Seleucia and sailed from there to Cyprus" (Acts 13:2–4).

The evangelization of the world depends, first of all, upon a revival of prayer. Even deeper than the need for workers is the need for prevailing prayer on behalf of those already laboring on our mission fields.

Pray that mission work may be done in a spirit of waiting upon God, hearing the voice of the Spirit, and sending workers out with fasting and prayer. Pray that in our churches, our missionary interests may be directed by the power of the Holy Spirit and concentrated prayer. It is a Spirit-filled, praying church that will send out Spirit-filled, praying missionaries, equipped to invade the Enemy's territory.

How to Pray: Take Time

"I am a man of prayer" (Psalm 109:4).

"We will give our attention to prayer and the ministry of the word" (Acts 6:4).

"Do not be quick with your mouth, do not be hasty in your heart to utter anything before God. God is in heaven and you are on earth, so let your words be few" (Ecclesiastes 5:2).

Time is one of the primary standards of value. The time we give a thing is proof of the interest and value we place on it.

We need time with God in order to realize His presence, to wait for Him to make himself known, to consider and feel the needs we ask for, to take our place in Christ, and to pray until we truly believe we have received what we ask. Take time in prayer and receive blessing and provision for the mission work of the church.

Your Own Prayer Requests

DAY TEN
What to Pray: For God's Spirit on Our Missionaries

"But you will receive power when the Holy Spirit comes on you; and you will be my witnesses in Jerusalem, and in all Judea and Samaria, and to the ends of the earth" (Acts 1:8).

What the world needs today is not only more missionaries but the outpouring of God's Spirit on all those He has sent out to work for Him in the foreign fields.

God always gives His servants power equal to the work He asks of them. Think of the vastness and difficulty of this work. Most fields are under the power and sway of the enemy of our souls. Missionaries enter into Satan's strongholds. Before any significant work can be done, these powers must be broken down. Spiritual warfare is the order of the day. We must pray for those who have made it their life's work to face these difficulties head on and to minister to those who in many cases have never heard the name of Jesus, much less know anything of the Gospel. The work of prayer for missionaries is not easy. It takes dedication, concentration, and persistence. Do not give up the fight. God is with you.

How to Pray: Trusting God's Faithfulness

"Let us hold unswervingly to the hope we profess, for he who promised is faithful" (Hebrews 10:23).

Think of God's promises to His Son concerning His kingdom, to the church concerning the lost, to His servants concerning their ministry, and to you concerning your prayer life. Then pray in the assurance that He is faithful; He waits for prayer and faith so that He can answer and fulfill every request. "Faithful is he that calls you [to pray], who also will do [what He has promised]" (1 Thessalonians 5:24 KJV).

Take up individual missionaries that you know; make yourself one with them, and pray until you know that you are heard. Intercede on their behalf. There may be times and places where they are unable to pray and count on those at home to bridge the gap!

Your Own Prayer Requests

DAY ELEVEN
What to Pray: For More Laborers

"Ask the Lord of the harvest, therefore, to send out workers into his harvest field" (Matthew 9:38).

What a remarkable call of the Lord Jesus for help from His followers in filling the need for workers. Again, because of the strongholds of Satan in these lands, it is not an easy task to get young people to answer the call and to go out. It is truly through prayer that we can break through this barrier. Our text proves that God wants us to pray for laborers, and if He wants us to pray, He will hear us, and He will answer.

Pray for the young people studying in the theological seminaries, the missionary training centers, and Bible institutes, that they may have the courage and determination to prepare themselves and equip themselves for this great effort—the evangelization of the world. Encourage the faithful in your churches to cooperate in the financial support of those who are willing to go. Raise up prayer warriors who will without fail support the youth who give themselves to the fields that are white unto harvest.

How to Pray: By Faith, Doubting Nothing

" 'Have faith in God,' Jesus answered. 'I tell you the truth, if anyone says to this mountain, "Go, throw yourself into the sea," and does not doubt in his heart but believes that what he says will happen, it will be done for him' " (Mark 11:22–23).

Have faith in God! Ask Him to make himself known to you as the faithful, mighty God, who works all things out for His glory. You will be encouraged to believe that He can provide suitable and sufficient laborers for all the fields that need them, however impossible this might appear—but remember, nothing is done without prayer and faith.

Apply this wherever and whenever a good laborer is needed. The work is God's. He can give the appropriate worker for the appropriate field of service. But He must be asked. This is the method He has chosen. We must wait on Him and ask for laborers.

Your Own Prayer Requests

DAY TWELVE

What to Pray: For the Spirit to Convince the World of Sin

"But I tell you the truth: It is for your good that I am going away. Unless I go away, the Counselor will not come to you; but if I go, I will send him to you. When he comes, he will convict the world of guilt in regard to sin and righteousness and judgment" (John 16:7–8).

Christ's coming, death, and resurrection was to take away sin. The first work of the Holy Spirit is to convict the world of sin. Without conviction there is no repentance. And without repentance there is no salvation. Unless the Spirit moves to convict and convince of sin, no deep or abiding revival and no powerful conversion is possible. Pray that the Gospel may be preached in such power that all may see how they have rejected and crucified Christ afresh, and that they may cry out, "What shall we do?"

How to Pray: Stir Yourself Up to Take Hold of God's Strength

"Let them come to me for refuge; let them make peace with me, yes, let them make peace with me" (Isaiah 27:5).

"No one calls on your name or strives to lay hold of you; for you have hidden your face from us and made us waste away because of our sins" (Isaiah 64:7).

"For this reason I remind you to fan into flame the gift of God, which is in you through the laying on of my hands" (2 Timothy 1:6).

Appropriate God's strength. God is a Spirit. We cannot take hold of Him and keep Him with us but by the Spirit. Take refuge in God and secure from Him what He has promised: conviction of sin. Pray for the power of the Spirit to convince His people as well as the lost of their sins.

There is no effective prayer apart from the Spirit. Give your whole heart to Him in prayer and faith that He will work and reveal to those for whom you pray the true state of their hearts and their need to confess their sins and be made right with God.

Your Own Prayer Requests

DAY THIRTEEN
What to Pray: For the Spirit of Fire

"Those who are left in Zion, who remain in Jerusalem, will be called holy, all who are recorded among the living in Jerusalem. The LORD will wash away the filth of the women of Zion; he will cleanse the bloodstains from Jerusalem by a spirit of judgment and a spirit of fire" (Isaiah 4:3–4).

A washing by fire! A cleansing by judgment! He that has passed through this fire will be called holy. The blessing for the world, the power of the work of intercession that will avail, depends upon the spiritual state of the church. That state can only be elevated as sin is discovered and repented of. Judgment must begin at the house of God. There must be conviction of sin before there can be sanctification. Call upon God to pour out His Spirit as a spirit of judgment and a spirit of fire—to reveal and consume sin in His people.

How to Pray: In the Name of Christ

"And I will do whatever you ask in my name, so that the Son may bring glory to the Father. You may ask me for anything in my name, and I will do it" (John 14:13–14).

Ask what you will in the name of your Redeemer. He waits to grant your request. Ask what He has promised, what He died for, that sin may be put away from among His people. Ask for a spirit of conviction of sin, for a spirit of fire. We cannot go wrong when we pray the Scriptures. We know we pray according to His will. He would prepare His people to minister to the world, and this is impossible as long as sin is present. Ask in faith; ask in His name. Pray that the church may prepare itself to be effective in its ministry to the world.

Your Own Prayer Requests

DAY FOURTEEN
What to Pray: For the Church of the Future

"We will tell the next generation the praiseworthy deeds of the LORD, his power, and the wonders he has done. He decreed statutes for Jacob and established the law in Israel, which he commanded our forefathers to teach their children, so the next generation would know them, even the children yet to be born, and they in turn would tell their children. Then they would put their trust in God and would not forget his deeds but would keep his commands" (Psalm 78:4–7).

"For I will pour water on the thirsty land, and streams on the dry ground; I will pour out my Spirit on your offspring, and my blessing on your descendants" (Isaiah 44:3).

We must pray for the generations who will follow us. Unless the Word of God, the knowledge of the character of God, and the message of the Gospel are taught to our children and our children's children, what will come of the generations that follow? We can pray with relative ease for our own children, but we must think too of the young children in our churches, our schools, our neighborhoods, and pray for them and all their teachers and instructors and leaders at work among them; that whatever they do, Christ may be honored and the Holy Spirit gain entrance into their lives. The future of the church and the nation depend on it.

How to Pray: With the Whole Heart

"May he give you the desire of your heart and make all your plans succeed. We will shout for joy when you are victorious and will lift up our banners in the name of our God. May the LORD grant all your requests" (Psalm 20:4–5).

"You have granted him the desire of his heart and have not withheld the request of his lips" (Psalm 21:2).

"I call with all my heart; answer me, O LORD, and I will obey your decrees" (Psalm 119:145).

Prayer for future generations is crucial, and God desires to answer our supplications. He lives to hear and grant every petition with regard to souls and their eternal destiny. Each time we pray, the whole infinite God is there to hear us. He asks, as well, that in each prayer we pray, the whole person will be there too; that we will cry unto Him with our whole heart. Christ gave himself to God for us, and so He takes very seriously our call to Him for help. If once we seek God with our whole heart, we will see the difference between this and perfunctory, ritualistic prayers. The whole heart will be in every

...ith which we come to God. Pray with your whole heart
..or those who will follow us.

Your Own Prayer Requests

DAY FIFTEEN
What to Pray: For the Schools and Colleges

" 'As for me, this is my covenant with them,' says the LORD.
'My Spirit, who is on you, and my words that I have put in your
mouth will not depart from your mouth, or from the mouths of
your children, or from the mouths of their descendants from this
time on and forever,' says the LORD" (Isaiah 59:21).

The future of the church, the nation, and the world
depends—to an extent we scarcely conceive of—on the education
of our youth. The church may be seeking to evangelize the lost,
while it is giving up on its own children to secular and material-
istic influences. Pray for your schools and colleges. Pray for the
faculty, those who most influence the young in these halls of
learning. The church has an awesome responsibility to lay a foundation for these young people before they are sent away to hear
every form of half-truth and false teaching, every doctrine and

philosophy of man. May the church also realize its responsibility to pray and support these young people, guiding them to God's truth, and enabling them to make wise choices. Pray too for godly teachers, even in the secular schools.

How to Pray: Not Limiting God

"How often they rebelled against him in the desert and grieved him in the wasteland! Again and again they put God to the test; they vexed the Holy One of Israel. They did not remember his power—the day he redeemed them from the oppressor" (Psalm 78:40–42).

"And he did not do many miracles there because of their lack of faith" (Matthew 13:58).

"Is anything too hard for the LORD?" (Genesis 18:14).

"Ah, Sovereign LORD, you have made the heavens and the earth by your great power and outstretched arm. Nothing is too hard for you."

"I am the LORD, the God of all mankind. Is anything too hard for me?" (Jeremiah 32:17, 27).

Above everything, beware of limiting God—not only by unbelief but also by imagining that you know what He can do. Expect the unexpected—more than you could ask or think. Each time you intercede, be quiet first—listen and worship. Think of all He can do, of all He delights to do for His children, of your place in Christ, your identity with Him.

Your Own Prayer Requests

DAY SIXTEEN

What to Pray: For the Power of the Holy Spirit in our Sunday Schools

"But this is what the LORD says: 'Yes, captives will be taken from warriors, and plunder retrieved from the fierce; I will contend with those who contend with you, and your children I will save'" (Isaiah 49:25).

Every part of the work of God's church is His work. Prayer is the confession that He will work in answer to our prayers. One of the often neglected ministries in the church is the Sunday school. This is not a place to leave your children merely so that you can attend the worship service. Sunday school should be a place of learning, a place of prayer, a place of instruction in the things of God. Often there is a shortage of volunteers to teach and help in this ministry. We must come to understand how vital it is and how desperately important to the forming of the future leaders of our churches. Pray for teachers, qualified teachers, those who are enthused about the Word of God and awed at the preciousness of children. Pray for the children, that they will be encouraged to attend, desire to learn, and that they will retain what they have learned. Pray for an outpouring of the Holy Spirit on our Sunday schools so that our children may be nurtured and instructed while their minds and hearts are receptive. Pray for the salvation of the children.

How to Pray: Boldly

"Therefore, since we have a great high priest who has gone through the heavens, Jesus the Son of God, let us hold firmly to the faith we profess. Let us then approach the throne of grace with confidence, so that we may receive mercy and find grace to help us in our time of need" (Hebrews 4:14, 16).

We can approach the throne with confidence because we know that God delights to hear our prayers. Because of Jesus' sacrifice, we are accepted in Him. We are heard. Let us pray for our children with all boldness and confidence that God desires to bless them and use them. Let us persevere, realizing the value and importance of our subject. The more we pray the more we will learn how to pray, and to believe, and to expect an answer with increasing hope and confidence. Hold fast your assurance; it is at God's command you come before Him as an intercessor. Intercede for the Sunday schools and for the children who attend them.

Your Own Prayer Requests

DAY SEVENTEEN
What to Pray: For Those in Authority

"I urge, then, first of all, that requests, prayers, intercession and thanksgiving be made for everyone—for kings and all those in authority, that we may live peaceful and quiet lives in all god-liness and holiness" (1 Timothy 2:1–2).

What faith in the power of prayer! At the time this text was written it was a few weak and despised Christians that were expected to influence the mighty Roman emperors and help in securing peace and quietness. But their faith in prayer was what made the difference. It wasn't their own strength or power or influence but that of the Holy Spirit. And so must we pray for our country, our president, his cabinet, our governors, and all those who rule in the affairs of men, that they might rule with integrity and in the fear of God. When God's people unite, they can count upon their prayers affecting all that is done, seen and unseen. Let us pray in obedience to God's Word and be thankful for our freedoms and privileges.

How to Pray: As a Sweet-Smelling Offering to God

"Another angel, who had a golden censer, came and stood at the altar. He was given much incense to offer, with the prayers of all the saints, on the golden altar before the throne. The smoke of the incense, together with the prayers of the saints, went up before God from the angel's hand. Then the angel took the censer, filled it with fire from the altar, and hurled it on the earth; and there came peals of thunder, rumblings, flashes of lightning and an earthquake" (Revelation 8:3–5).

Not only is prayer a sweet-smelling offering to God, it is powerful and effective on the earth. God works through the prayers of His people. The prayers that reach heaven have their share in the history of this earth. We need to take our prayer time as seriously as God takes it. Intercession is not a ritual or a pastime. It is the power of God among men. Be assured that your prayers enter God's presence and are used for His glory.

Your Own Prayer Requests

DAY EIGHTEEN
What to Pray: For Peace

"I urge, then, first of all, that requests, prayers, intercession and thanksgiving be made for everyone—for kings and all those in authority, that we may live peaceful and quiet lives in all godliness and holiness. This is good, and pleases God our Savior, who wants all men to be saved and to come to a knowledge of the truth" (1 Timothy 2:1–4).

"He makes wars cease to the ends of the earth; he breaks the bow and shatters the spear, he burns the shields with fire. 'Be still, and know that I am God; I will be exalted among the nations, I will be exalted in the earth'" (Psalm 46:9–10).

The military armaments in which the nations find their pride is an awesome thought! What is worse are the possibilities of what the evil passions of men might at any moment bring about! It is a prospect of suffering and desolation even upon the innocent and the young. But God can, in answer to the prayers of His people, give divine peace. Let us pray for it and for the rule of righteousness on which alone peace can be established.

How to Pray: With Understanding

"So what shall I do? I will pray with my spirit, but I will also pray with my mind [my understanding]; I will sing with my spirit, but I will also sing with my mind [my understanding]" (1 Corinthians 14:15).

We need to pray from our spirit as the vehicle of the intercession of God's Spirit if we are to take hold of God in faith and power. And we need to pray with understanding if we are to truly enter deeply into the needs we bring before Him. Take time to grasp intelligently each subject, its nature and extent, the urgency of the request, the grounds for the certainty of God's promise as revealed in His Word. Let the mind influence the heart. Pray with understanding and with the mind of the Spirit.

Your Own Prayer Requests

DAY NINETEEN

What to Pray: For the Descent of the Holy Spirit on All Christendom

"Having a form of godliness but denying its power" (2 Timothy 3:5).

"These are the words of him who holds the seven spirits of God and the seven stars. I know your deeds; you have a reputation of being alive, but you are dead" (Revelation 3:1).

There are millions of so-called nominal Christians—Christians in name only. They say they are Christians, but they deny the power of God. Their lives are dull and without spiritual vitality. Formality, ritual, performance, worldliness, ungodliness, rejection of service for Christ, ignorance, and indifference all describe this group. We pray for the lost, but do we also pray for those bearing Christ's name who are in worse shape than some who do not claim the name of Christ in any form?

If we think much about it, we would say it is a severe problem and an issue that needs a great amount of work and prayer.

How to Pray: In Deep Stillness of Soul

"My soul finds rest in God alone; my salvation comes from him" (Psalm 62:1).

Prayer has its power in God alone. The nearer a man comes to God, the deeper he enters into God's will. The more he takes hold of God, the more power he has in prayer.

God must reveal himself. We as mere men must take time to receive this revelation. If it pleases Him to make himself known,

He can make the heart and mind very conscious of His presence. Our posture must be that of reverence, of quiet waiting and adoration.

As you intercede for all those for whom Christianity is a social pastime, be still before God and know His mind and heart. You will receive the power and understanding that is needed to pray with passion for these who are as lost as the pagan.

Your Own Prayer Requests

DAY TWENTY
What to Pray: For God's Spirit on the Heathen

"See, they will come from afar—some from the north, some from the west, some from the region of Aswan" (Isaiah 49:12).

"Envoys will come from Egypt; Cush will submit herself to God" (Psalm 68:31).

"The least of you will become a thousand, the smallest a mighty nation. I am the LORD; in its time I will do this swiftly" (Isaiah 60:22).

Typically, the heathen are those who have never heard the

gospel of Jesus Christ, or if they have heard it, they have rejected it. Many of these have been born into other religions and practiced them all their lives. We usually think of the heathen as people in foreign countries, but anyone who rejects the Gospel out of hand could be called a heathen. Pray especially for those who are yet without the Word of God. There are many in the Far East who have never heard and some in the darkest recesses of Africa. Christ gave His life for all of these, and we must be willing to give ours. The least we can do is intercede for them in prayer.

If you have not yet begun, begin with this simple monthly school of intercession. The ten minutes you give will soon make you feel it is not enough. God's Spirit will draw you on. Persevere, however weak you feel. Ask God to give you some country or tribe or people group to pray for. Can anything be nobler than to do as Christ did? Give your life for the heathen.

How to Pray: With Confident Expectation of an Answer

"Call to me and I will answer you and tell you great and unsearchable things you do not know" (Jeremiah 33:3).

"This is what the Sovereign LORD says: 'Once again I will yield to the plea of the house of Israel and do this for them: I will make their people as numerous as sheep'" (Ezekiel 36:37).

Both texts refer to promises made, but their fulfillment depends upon prayer: God must be inquired of to do it.

Pray for the fulfillment of God's promises to His Son and to His church. Pray for the salvation of the heathen—particularly those who have truly never heard the Gospel. Plead God's promises. Claim what He says He will do in response to our intercessory prayer.

Your Own Prayer Requests

DAY TWENTY-ONE
What to Pray: For God's Spirit on the Jews

"And I will pour out on the house of David and the inhabitants of Jerusalem a spirit of grace and supplication. They will look on me, the one they have pierced, and they will mourn for him as one mourns for an only child, and grieve bitterly for him as one grieves for a firstborn son" (Zechariah 12:10).

"Brothers, my heart's desire and prayer to God for the Israelites is that they may be saved" (Romans 10:1).

Pray for the Jews. Their return to the God of their fathers stands connected in a way we cannot understand, with wonderful blessing to the church and with the coming of our Lord Jesus. It is tempting to think that God has foreordained all this and that we cannot hasten it. But in a divine and mysterious way God has connected the fulfillment of His promises with our prayers. His Spirit's intercession in us is God's forerunner of blessing. Pray for

Israel and for the work being done among her people. We can also pray, "Amen. Even so, come, Lord Jesus!"

How to Pray: With the Intercession of the Holy Spirit

"In the same way, the Spirit helps us in our weakness. We do not know what we ought to pray for, but the Spirit himself intercedes for us with groans that words cannot express" (Romans 8:26).

Even when you lack knowledge or feel weak and ineffective, the Holy Spirit indwells you and intercedes through you. Yield yourself to His leading. Make a habit of it. He will help your inadequacies in prayer. Plead the promises of God even when you do not see how they are to be fulfilled or where they fit in. God knows the mind of the Spirit; He makes intercession for the saints according to the will of God. Pray with the simplicity of a child; pray with the holy awe and reverence of one in whom God's Spirit dwells and prays.

Your Own Prayer Requests

DAY TWENTY-TWO
What to Pray—For All Who Are Suffering

"Remember those in prison as if you were their fellow prisoners, and those who are mistreated as if you yourselves were suffering" (Hebrews 13:3).

We live in a world of suffering. Jesus sacrificed everything to identify himself with it—with them. Let us seek to do our part in identifying with those who suffer, empathizing with them in their grief and pain—the persecuted believers around the world, the famine-stricken millions in Africa, the poverty and wretchedness of the developing countries, and so much more; what suffering among those who know God as well as those who do not know Him. Then in smaller circles, in many homes and hearts in our own country, in our own neighborhoods, prayer is needed. There are children who suffer abuse, parents who struggle to provide for their families. Many need our help and comfort. Let us seek them out and pray for a heart that weeps with them. It will stir us to pray, to work, to hope, to love more than we do. And in ways and at times we least expect, God will hear our prayers. He is at work even before we ask.

How to Pray—Praying Always, Not Fainting

"Then Jesus told his disciples a parable to show them that they should always pray and not give up" (Luke 18:1).

Do you believe prayer is the solution for this sinful world? If you do, you will also see the need for unceasing prayer! The greatness of the task would overwhelm us and cause us to despair were it not for God's promise of the Holy Spirit's assistance. What can our ten minutes of intercession avail? Even ten minutes is better than no prayer, but after ten minutes we will begin to sense the burden of the Spirit and we will find that more time is needed before we even scratch the surface of the need. God is calling and preparing us every day to give our life to prayer. Give yourself to God for the sake of others and you will not regret that you did. God's work is our work. Let us go to Him with expectant hearts, full of faith and boldness. The Enemy of our souls will not have his way if we pray always, led by the Holy Spirit. It is possible to pray always and not to faint! Don't give up!

Your Own Prayer Requests

DAY TWENTY-THREE
What to Pray—For the Holy Spirit in Your Own Work

"To this end I labor, struggling with all his energy, which so powerfully works in me" (Colossians 1:29).

Each of us has our own work to do each day, however secular or ministry-oriented it may be. It is where God has placed us. We are ministers wherever we are. We are witnesses of His grace and mercy. Make your place of work a place of intercession for those around you. Paul labored, striving according to the working of God in him. Remember, God is not only the Creator but also the Sustainer of all. You can do your daily work effectively only in His strength and by His working in you through the Spirit. Be an example of hard work and patient understanding of the trials and difficulties of others. Co-workers will sense that you have a source of strength and energy that they do not. This can be a platform of testimony for you.

Use your spare moments to pray for those who are over you and any who may work for you. Especially remember those who labor in the church, however solitary or unknown they may be.

How to Pray—In God's Very Presence

"Come near to God and he will come near to you. Wash your hands, you sinners, and purify your hearts, you double-minded" (James 4:8).

The nearness of God gives confidence and power in prayer. He is never far from us, but waits for us to draw near to Him, to confess any sin and to be cleansed afresh. When our hearts are pure before Him we can focus on the needs of others. It is easy to pray in faith when we know God is near and waiting and there is nothing between us and Him.

When God first draws us into the school of intercession, it is as much for us as it is for others. It trains us to love and wait and pray and believe. Learn to rely on His presence, to be assured of it. Then bring your work to Him, your co-workers, your successes, and your failures. Intercede for those souls who do not know Him, but who know you and with whom you are in contact every day. Your compassion for them will grow, and God will equip you to minister to them in their times of special need.

Your Own Prayer Requests

DAY TWENTY-FOUR
What to Pray—For the Spirit on Your Own Congregation

"He told them, 'This is what is written: The Christ will suffer and rise from the dead on the third day, and repentance and forgiveness of sins will be preached in his name to all nations, *beginning at Jerusalem.* You are witnesses of these things. I am going to send you what my Father has promised; but *stay in the city* until you have been clothed with power from on high'" (Luke 24:46–49, emphasis added).

Each one of us is connected with some congregation or circle of believers. They are to us the part of Christ's body with which we come into most direct contact. They have a special claim on our intercession. Let it be a settled matter between God and you that you are to labor in prayer on its behalf. Pray for the minister and all layleaders or workers within it. Pray for the believers according to their needs. Pray for the conversion of unbelievers.

Pray for the power of the Spirit to manifest itself in your services and outreaches. Join yourself with others to pray for specific petitions that are brought to your attention. Let intercession be a definite work in your midst, carried on as systematically as the preaching, the worship, and the Sunday school classes. And when you pray, *expect* answers.

How to Pray—Continually

"I have posted watchmen on your walls, O Jerusalem; they will never be silent day or night. You who call on the LORD, give yourselves no rest" (Isaiah 62:6).

"And will not God bring about justice for his chosen ones, who cry out to him day and night? Will he keep putting them off? I tell you, he will see that they get justice, and quickly" (Luke 18:7–8).

"Night and day we pray most earnestly that we may see you again and supply what is lacking in your faith" (1 Thessalonians 3:10).

"The widow who is really in need and left all alone puts her hope in God and continues night and day to pray and to ask God for help" (1 Timothy 5:5).

When the glory of God, and the love of Christ, and the need of souls are revealed to us, the fire of this unceasing intercession will begin to burn in us. It will not be hard to pray every time these people and these needs come to mind. If we remain in an attitude of prayer, the Holy Spirit will bring to mind needs as they arise. When we awake at night, we will know for whom we should pray. Prayer is ongoing in the life of the intercessor. It really has no beginning and no end. In the power of the Spirit it is not a tiresome thing, but a source of energy and satisfaction.

Your Own Prayer Requests

DAY TWENTY-FIVE
What to Pray—For More Conversions

"Therefore he is able to save completely those who come to God through him, because he always lives to intercede for them" (Hebrews 7:25).

"We . . . will give our attention to prayer and the ministry of the word.

"So the word of God spread. The number of disciples in Jerusalem increased rapidly, and a large number of priests became obedient to the faith" (Acts 6:4, 7).

Christ's power to save, and save completely, depends on His unceasing intercession. After the apostles withdrew themselves to concentrated prayer, the number of the disciples multiplied rapidly.

As we in our day give ourselves to intercession, we will also see more conversions. Let this be our focus. Christ is exalted to grant repentance and salvation. The church exists for the divine purpose of growth in faith and in numbers. Let us not be ashamed to confess our sin and weakness, and then to cry to God for more souls to be saved both in our midst and in countries where His Word is not preached and people cling to false gods and die without hope.

How to Pray—In Deepest Humility

" 'Yes, Lord,' she said, 'but even the dogs eat the crumbs that fall from their masters' table.' Then Jesus answered, 'Woman, you have great faith! Your request is granted.' And her daughter was healed from that very hour" (Matthew 15:27–28).

You feel unworthy to pray. You question whether you are praying effectively. Even when you feel this way, come before Him and tell Him how you feel. This is true humility. You are not seeking for yourself, but for others. You are trusting His grace and mercy, not your merits or influence. It is the beginning of a great faith, and an answer is forthcoming. The woman reminded the Lord that the dogs are allowed the crumbs that fall from the table. Let that be your plea as you persevere for someone who is outside the circle of faith or outside the hearing of the Gospel. Do not let your unworthiness hinder you from trusting God's faithfulness and mercy toward someone less fortunate than you.

Your Own Prayer Requests

DAY TWENTY-SIX
What to Pray—For the Holy Spirit on Young Converts

"When they arrived, they prayed for them that they might receive the Holy Spirit, because the Holy Spirit had not yet come upon any of them; they had simply been baptized into the name of the Lord Jesus" (Acts 8:15–16).

"Now it is God who makes both us and you stand firm in Christ. He anointed us, set his seal of ownership on us, and put his Spirit in our hearts as a deposit, guaranteeing what is to come" (2 Corinthians 1:21–22).

Many new converts remain weak; many fall into sin; many backslide entirely. If you pray for the church, its growth in holiness and devotion to God's service, pray especially for the young converts. Many stand alone, surrounded by temptation; many have no teaching on the Spirit in them and the power of God to establish them. Some are without support of family or friends. Some are in countries that are closed to the Gospel, where Satan has a stronghold. When you pray for the power of the Spirit in the church, pray in particular that every young or new convert may know that he may claim and receive the fullness of the Spirit in his life.

How to Pray—Without Ceasing

"As for me, far be it from me that I should sin against the Lord by failing to pray for you. And I will teach you the way that is good and right" (1 Samuel 12:23).

We are sinning against the Lord if we cease to pray for others. When we begin to see how absolutely indispensable intercession is, just as much our responsibility as loving God or believing in Christ, and how we are called and bound to it as believers, we will be convinced that to cease our intercession is a serious sin. Let us ask for grace to take our place as priests with joy and give our life to bring down the blessing of heaven on those who depend on our prayers and supplications.

Your Own Prayer Requests

DAY TWENTY-SEVEN
What to Pray—That God's People May Realize Their Calling

"I will make you into a great nation and I will bless you; I will make your name great, and you will be a blessing. I will bless those who bless you, and whoever curses you I will curse; and all peoples on earth will be blessed through you" (Genesis 12:2–3).

"May God be gracious to us and bless us and make his face shine upon us, that your ways may be known on earth, your salvation among all nations" (Psalm 67:1–2).

Abraham was only blessed that he might be a blessing to all the earth. Israel prays for blessing that God may be known among all nations. Every believer, just as Abraham was, is only blessed that he may carry God's blessing to the world.

Plead with God that His people may know this: that every believer is to live for the interests of God and His kingdom. If this truth were preached and believed and practiced, what a revolution it would bring to our churches and our mission fields. What a host of willing intercessors we would have. Ask God to reveal this by the Holy Spirit.

How to Pray—As One Who Has Accepted for Himself What He Asks for Others

"As I began to speak, the Holy Spirit came on them as he had come on us at the beginning. So if God gave them the same gift as he gave us, who believed in the Lord Jesus Christ, who was I to think that I could oppose God?" (Acts 11:15, 17).

When God has blessed us and met our needs, we are encouraged and emboldened to ask the same for others. Let any thought of your own weakness or shortcomings only make you more urgent in prayer. As His child, you will be heard, many will be helped, and your own faith will be strengthened.

Your Own Prayer Requests

DAY TWENTY-EIGHT
What to Pray—That All God's People May Know the Holy Spirit

"And I will ask the Father, and he will give you another Counselor to be with you forever—the Spirit of truth. The world cannot accept him, because it neither sees him nor knows him. But you know him, for he lives with you and will be in you" (John 14:16–17).

"Do you not know that your body is a temple of the Holy Spirit, who is in you, whom you have received from God? You are not your own" (1 Corinthians 6:19).

The Holy Spirit is the power of God for the salvation of men. He only works as He dwells in the church. He is given to enable believers to live as God would have them live, in the full experience and witness of Him who saves completely.

Pray that all God's people will come to know the Holy Spirit and His function in their lives. He will reveal Jesus to us and empower us to be His witnesses. We cannot expect to live as effective Christians in prayer or in service without having the fullness of the Holy Spirit in our lives. If you believe in the Trinity, do not neglect the Holy Spirit.

How to Pray—Laboring Fervently in Prayer

"Epaphras, who is one of you and a servant of Christ Jesus, sends greetings. He is always wrestling in prayer for you, that you may stand firm in all the will of God, mature and fully assured" (Colossians 4:12).

To a healthy person, work is a delight, and that person works hard at what interests him. The believer who is healthy—has a clear conscience, a pure heart, and a desire to serve God—labors fervently in prayer. True intercession is fervent prayer for others: that they might stand perfect and complete in all the will of God; that they may know what God expects of them; how He calls them to live; and that they might be led by and walk in the Holy Spirit. Labor fervently in prayer that all God's children may know this.

Your Own Prayer Requests

DAY TWENTY-NINE
What to Pray—For the Spirit of Intercession

"You did not choose me, but I chose you and appointed you to go and bear fruit—fruit that will last. Then the Father will give you whatever you ask in my name" (John 15:16).

"Until now you have not asked for anything in my name. Ask and you will receive, and your joy will be complete.... In that day you will ask in my name" (John 16:24, 26).

If nothing else, our school of intercession has taught us how little we have prayed in the name of Jesus. He promised His disciples that in the day the Holy Spirit came upon them they would ask in His name. Until we know and understand the work of the Spirit in the life of the intercessor, we grieve the lack of power in prayer. First we lack motivation, then we say we have no time, then we seem to sense we are getting nowhere. But if the Holy Spirit dwells in us, intercession will be natural to us. We will learn to live in His fullness, and to yield ourselves to His intercessory work through us. The church and the world need nothing so much as a mighty Spirit of intercession to call down the power of God on earth. Then we will know His presence as never before and see true revival in our midst.

How to Pray—Abiding in Christ

"If you remain in me and my words remain in you, ask whatever you wish, and it will be given you" (John 15:7).

Our acceptance with God and our access to Him is only possible through Christ. As we consciously abide in Him we have the freedom to ask whatever we wish—because our old nature has been put to death and our requests are in harmony with our new nature, which is in alignment with the will of God. If we remain in this fellowship, our intercession will be effective. We will not have to be concerned about whether we are being heard and whether our requests will be granted. If we are in the will of God, we can be assured of the answer.

Your Own Prayer Requests

DAY THIRTY
What to Pray—For the Holy Spirit With the Word of God

"For we know, brothers loved by God, that he has chosen you, because our gospel came to you not simply with words, but also with power, with the Holy Spirit and with deep conviction. You know how we lived among you for your sake" (1 Thessalonians 1:5).

"It was revealed to them that they were not serving themselves but you, when they spoke of the things that have now been told you by those who have preached the gospel to you by the Holy Spirit sent from heaven" (1 Peter 1:12).

The Word of God is circulated without much difficulty in countries where there is freedom of religion. Most sermons are preached based on the Word of God—or should be. Bibles—including various versions—are being read in homes and in private schools. The Word is powerful and will accomplish what God intends in each place, but how important it is to intercede in these places, that the Holy Spirit will attend the Word in power through those who are filled with the Spirit and who read the Word with the eyes of the Spirit's understanding. Pray for Bible circulation in countries where it is restricted or even prohibited, but pray too for the accompaniment of the Holy Spirit in minds and hearts and in preaching and teaching and reading, that its full effect may be felt in every place. Let every mention of the Word of God awaken intercessory prayer.

How to Pray—Watching and Praying

"Devote yourselves to prayer, being watchful and thankful. And pray for us, too, that God may open a door for our message, so that we may proclaim the mystery of Christ, for which I am in chains" (Colossians 4:2–3).

Do you see how everything depends upon God and prayer? As long as He lives and loves and hears and works, as long as there are souls with hearts closed to the Word of God, as long as there is work to be done in carrying the Word to the ends of the earth—pray without ceasing. "Continue in prayer, watching in the same with thanksgiving." These words are for every Christian. No one is exempt.

Your Own Prayer Requests

DAY THIRTY-ONE
What to Pray—For the Spirit of Christ in His People

"I am the vine; you are the branches. If a man remains in me and I in him, he will bear much fruit; apart from me you can do nothing" (John 15:5).

"I have set you an example that you should do as I have done for you" (John 13:15).

As branches of the Vine, we are to be so like the Vine, so entirely identified with it, that all may see that we have the same nature, and life, and spirit. When we pray for the Spirit, let us not only think of a Spirit of *power*, but the very *disposition* and *temper* of Christ. Ask for and expect nothing less. Ask it for yourself and ask it for all God's children. This should be the deepest cry of our heart.

How to Pray—Striving in Prayer

"I urge you, brothers, by our Lord Jesus Christ and by the love of the Spirit, to join me in my struggle by praying to God for me" (Romans 15:30).

"I want you to know how much I am struggling for you and for those at Laodicea, and for all who have not met me personally" (Colossians 2:1).

Paul asked his followers to join him in his trials by praying for him. All the powers of evil seek to hinder us in prayer. Prayer is a conflict with opposing forces. It requires the whole heart and all our strength. May God give us grace to strive in prayer for others, and may we all be blessed with many who pray also for us.

Your Own Prayer Requests

Change *Prayer* From *Discipline* to *Delight*

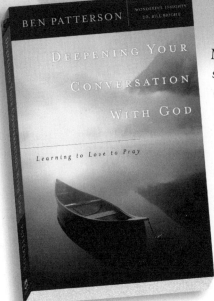

Most Christians know prayer is something they are supposed to do, so they dutifully spend a few moments a day praying. Yet, more often than that, they feel like they're checking an item off their spiritual to-do list rather than having a meaningful encounter with the Holy God.

In *Deepening Your Conversation With God*, Ben Patterson explores how he learned to start reveling in prayer, eagerly awaiting his next chance to pray. More than a "how to pray" book, this is a *"want to pray"* guide that nurtures a thirst in Christians for true communion with God. Readers are calling it life-changing!

Deepening Your Conversation with God
by Ben Patterson

◊ BETHANYHOUSE